D1474896

LEGAL THINKING

LEGAL THINKING

Its Limits and Tensions

WILLIAM READ

upp

University of Pennsylvania Press

Philadelphia · 1986

Library of Congress Cataloging-in-Publication Data

Read, William.
Legal thinking.

Includes index.
1. Law—Methodology. 2. Law—Philosophy. I. Title.
K212.R43 1986 340'.1 85-31448
ISBN 0-8122-8023-7 (alk. paper)

Printed in the United States of America

CONTENTS

CHAPTER TWO
Materials for Legal Thinking

CHAPTER THREE
Problems for Legal Thinking

PART TWO

TENSIONS IN LEGAL THINKING

CHAPTER FOUR

Tension Between Structures and Freedom Regarding What the Law Requires

CHAPTER FIVE

Tension Between Law and Morals

CHAPTER SIX
Tension Between Norms and Facts

ACKNOWLEDGMENTS

The ideas of many English and American judges (most conspicuously, Justice Oliver Wendell Holmes) and of many legal and moral theorists (Hans Kelsen, H. L. A. Hart, John Rawls, and Ronald Dworkin, to name a few) helped to shape the concept of legal thinking offered in this book.

The support of the faculty, administration, and students of the University of Louisville Law School helped get it written. My colleague, Leonard Jaffee, read early versions and made valuable suggestions. Marilyn Peters guided the manuscript through its changes on her word processor. A generation of students pressed to have legal thinking made sensible.

The patience and encouragement of my wife, Dorothy Townsend Read, provided the day-to-day conditions that made this undertaking doable. And in its final stages, the perceptive editing of our daughter, Mary Read English, saved the manuscript from many infelicities. Those remaining are my own.

INTRODUCTION

Initially, this book was intended for beginning law students, and I hope that they will read it. But as the book developed, it changed from an effort simply to pass on what I believed I already knew to the more demanding undertaking of thinking through afresh what one does when one thinks legally. Thus, I hope those who read this book will include all who are interested in what we do when we think about legal problems.

A threshold question is whether legal thinking can be distinguished from other thinking. Obviously, I believe it can be, but not easily; and this book is an attempt to explain what makes thinking about legal problems a special kind of thinking with its own limits and tensions. To the next and harder question—Why bother?—my response is that lawyers and nonlawyers alike (and I argue that no participant in a legal system can avoid doing some legal thinking) do better legal thinking when they have thought about what they are doing. My own considerations of legal thinking lead me to make the effort to define its objective limits or boundaries, which are largely determined from outside our own minds, and, more ambitiously, to examine its subjective, energizing tensions, which we experience within our own minds.

The concept of legal thinking here presented employs a series of distinctions implicit in legal discourse but seldom made explicit. In brief, they contrast subjects and officials, norms and facts, abstract questions and situations, structures and freedom, law and morals, and respect for normative authority and prudence. The chapters of the book are elaborations of these distinctions.

My basic building block is a "legal norm": a statement, legal because it is backed by a government, and normative because it is about what ought to be. We do legal thinking when we think about at least one arguably legal norm and how it connects with a fact relevant to the norm's identity, meaning, applicability, or application. I use legal norms rather than legal rules in order to encompass "ought" statements not ordinarily called rules—such as legal principles and methods, and legally binding promises.

As used here, "legal system" means a normative system with a hierarchy of legal norms; lower norms are validated (made legally binding) by higher norms, and higher norms are particularized by lower norms (a contract is validated by the law of contracts, and the law of contracts is particularized by a contract). In addition, a legal system includes facts about or connecting with legal norms, the structures created and the freedom permitted in determining what the law requires, and the persons who think—as subjects, officials, advisers, or legislators—about legal problems involving such norms. And the term *law* includes all of the components of a legal system except those persons doing the legal thinking.

The first part of the book deals with the limits or bounds of legal thinking. These three chapters make the point that legal thinking is a limited sort of endeavor with limited objectives—an endeavor that can be identified, described, and distinguished from other kinds of thinking. One does legal thinking from a special point of view (determined by one's position in or in relation to a legal system), using normative and factual materials, about an abstract or situational problem concerning a legal norm.

The special points of view of legal thinking are the perspectives of (1) the subjects to whom the law applies, (2) the officials who apply the law to others, (3) those who advise others about legal problems, (4) the legislators who make new legal norms, and (5) the legal scholars who teach and write about the law (see Chapter 1). The normative materials used by these people are legal norms found in rules, principles, and methods and moral norms found in attitudes, obligations, and ideals; the factual materials are these people's perceptions about events and circumstances and their judgments about what is prudent in light of probable consequences to interests and values (see Chapter 2). The problems they consider are questions about the identity and meaning of legal norms in the abstract, and situations that entail determining the normative applicability and the actual application of legal norms to specific events (see Chapter 3).

In brief, the limits of legal thinking are marked by its points of view, its materials, and its problems—by who thinks about what and to what end. Being aware of and understanding these limits form the beginning of understanding legal thinking. But legal thinking in action is energized by several kinds of subjective tensions that make it more complex than is apparent from a description of its external boundaries. These tensions, which are discussed in the book's second part and can be summarized as pitting order against flexibility, take different forms at different stages of thinking about legal problems.

At the outset of a legal problem, when one is determining what the law requires, tension arises between the law's structures and the freedom the law permits to judge for oneself (see Chapter 4). Even after the differences between what is legal and illegal are clear, it still may be difficult to know what one ought to do, because the instructions of law and morals seem to differ (see Chapter 5). And, finally, when these tensions are resolved and it is clear what ought to be done, it still remains to be seen whether respect for the normative authority of the law or prudential concerns about factual consequences to interests or values will determine what is actually done (see Chapter 6).

Brief explanations are in order concerning my position in the debates about how law relates to morals and facts and my arguably unorthodox uses of the terms *freedom*, *morals*, and *values*.

I do not accept either natural law's claim that a norm's legal validity depends on the morality of its content (immoral laws are not laws at all) or legal realism's assertion that law is inseparable from fact (law is only what it does). And, while I do accept legal positivism's assumptions that a norm's legal validity depends on its backing, not its content, and that legal norms can be separated from moral norms and from facts (law is law), I also recognize that legal problems are seldom resolved by law alone. In short, my position is: law is law, but that is only the beginning in understanding legal thinking.

To get at how law, morals, and facts interact in legal thinking, I focus on the tensions described in the second part of the book. In a rough way, legal positivism is addressed in Chapter 4 (How do we know what is legal?), natural law in Chapter 5 (How do we reconcile what is legal with what is moral?), and legal realism in Chapter 6 (How do we reconcile what is legal and moral with what is prudent?). I do not, of course, claim that my tensions thesis is the only way to describe the interaction of law, morals, and facts in legal thinking.

The freedom I discuss in Chapter 4 is not moral, political, or social, but rather the legal freedom thrust on or left open to legal thinkers by how a legal system works. It results largely from what has been called the open texture of law. While it can involve morality, government power, and social order, its content depends not on individual rights but on the contents of particular legal problems. It occurs when thinkers are left to think for themselves. And it includes, perhaps controversially, the freedom of a subject to choose to disobey the law and to take the consequences.

In Chapter 5, I divide morals, as I do in Chapter 2, into positive morality, on the one hand, and ideals of justice and fairness on the other. I further divide positive morality into social attitudes (mores) and individual obligations; and I include in the latter both self-imposed obligations (conscience) and those imposed by one's positions (ethics). I accept the distinction in moral theory between social and critical morality but prefer to call the former "positive" morality in order to include not only social attitudes but also the actual obligations of conscience and position, and the latter "ideals" in order to make clear their nonpositivist origins.

I am also arguably unorthodox in my failure to include in

morals the idea of values, since the term may be used for what people believe to be moral. In Chapter 2, I use the word *value* to refer to what is in fact desired or wanted, which may or may not be what is considered morally worthwhile. I continue this usage in Chapter 6 by putting values on the factual side of norm-fact tension. I am concerned with the content or origin of values only as they illuminate how the process of valuing figures in legal thinking. For example, if a legally and morally binding contract turns out to be costly to me, I will experience less norm-value tension in choosing whether to abide by the contract if promise keeping outranks profit maximization in my value system. And my promise-keeping value may come from moral sources (my conscience or an ideal I hold about fairness) or from a self-regarding business interest in promises of this sort being kept.

Part One

LIMITS OF LEGAL THINKING

Chapter One

POINTS OF VIEW FOR LEGAL THINKING

The points of view from which we think set perhaps the most basic limits on how we think. Whether one is thinking as one who is required to accept a specific system of legal norms as a circumstance of life, like mortality, or as one who is free to speculate about what legal norms ought to be separates two quite disparate kinds of perspectives for legal thinking. The first perspective is that of a system's subjects and officials and their advisers; being participants in the system, they must accept its norms as givens. The second is that of legislators and legal scholars who are less restrained by this need (although legislators must, of course, respect limits on their legislative powers). The situational legal problems of the first group require real-life choices and decisions that connect legal norms with facts, whereas the more abstract legal problems of the second group permit freer, more inventive thinking.

Within the broad categories of those who think within and those who think about a legal system, differences exist depending on one's point of view. This chapter first deals with the several points of view of those who must accept existing legal norms as facts of life: a legal system's subjects seeking to live with and under its norms, its officials whose duty it is to enforce and apply these norms, and advisers helping others make their legal choices and decisions. The chapter then examines the more detached perspectives of legislators, and of those who teach and write about the law. In Europe, law graduates usually choose whether they will be judges, advisers, or legal scholars, and the choice is usually permanent. In the United States (and to a lesser extent, in Great Britain), it is much easier for law graduates to move around among being advisers, officials of various sorts, and law teachers—a mobility that sometimes obscures the differences in perspective examined in this chapter.

Subjects

According to anthropologists, a characteristic of true law, primitive or developed, is that it has teeth that can bite. Law from the point of view of those who may be bitten (its subjects) is a perspective shared at some times by almost everybody (the king in an absolute monarchy who stayed in his own realm would be an exception). And our legal thinking takes on special urgency when we envision the law being applied to ourselves.

As subjects, our thinking about the legal norms that govern us is characterized by self-concern, immediacy, and practicality. Unlike officials, advisers, legislators, and scholars, our mind sets are neither objective, vicarious, public, nor academic. For example, when experienced trial lawyers are themselves summoned as witnesses, they often are surprised at the intensity of their feelings when called on to answer questions under oath, particularly if the questioning is hostile.

Justice Holmes suggested that the clearest picture of law is through the eyes of a "bad man," concerned only with what he can get away with. This view may be too cynical, because we are often law abiding when we do not have to be: as when we obey a traffic signal or a speed limit, or even when we make out a tax return, in situations in which ignoring the law carries little danger. Nevertheless, Holmes's bad-man approach highlights important differences between the perspectives of subjects and officials, differences found in games as well as in law. By participating in a legal system or in a game, subjects or players tacitly agree to abide by official decisions, but they do not ordinarily assume responsibility for making close calls against themselves. This self-concern of even good subjects or players grows stronger as a rule's application to a given set of facts becomes less clear and as they become concerned that officials are making "bad calls" against them. We seem to have a natural propensity, fed by the emotional charge we feel when our own interests and values are at stake, to resolve doubts in our own favor and to find justification for our actions that will enhance our self-image. This propensity helps explain why legal systems and games need officials (as well as rules and professional advisers) who can supply objectivity and expertise for embattled subjects and players to aid them in coping with rules.

So far it has been assumed that subjects are simply those who experience the law—those who are governed by mandatory, existing laws, because of either their own consciences or enforcing officials. But this picture is incomplete. As will be discussed in a later section, the law also has a permissive, instrumental aspect that allows subjects to become informal lawmakers by entering into contracts, conveyances, incorporations, marriages, and the like. Through these transactions, ordinary citizens create new legal norms that are as much a part of law as are the externally imposed legal norms that punish crimes. Although contracts and conveyances require less official intervention than do incorporations and marriages, all of these legal acts are privately initiated.

The mandatory parts of law, such as rules against murder and requirements that we pay our taxes, are self-justifying; they are ends in themselves and thus have built-in imperatives. But the permissive parts of the law, such as legal norms enabling us to contract or marry, are simply a means to an end and so lack these built-in imperatives. For example, the very act of paying one's taxes has, in itself, a virtue that is lacking in the act of making a contract. Tax payment more closely resembles the performance than the making of a contract. The legal obligations that we take on by contracting or marrying are mandatory, but we have chosen to assume them. And in making this choice, we balance the anticipated benefits of the contract or marriage against its future obligations in a way that is quite different from the way most people balance the benefits and costs of committing murder or not paying their taxes.

Officials

We now move from those who may be bitten by the law to those who do the biting. Knowing how a legal system's officials think about its laws tells us more about how the system works than knowing how its subjects think, because the teeth of the law bite only when those officials put them in motion. And some legal philosophers (notably Hans Kelsen) assert that laws are really addressed to officials rather than to subjects. For example, they would translate the law against murder as follows: If A kills his neighbor B under circumstances in which A mistakes B for a burglar, then it is the duty of certain officials of A's community to set in motion certain procedures, which will ultimately result in A being punished or exonerated. While A's state of mind when he shoots B is a relevant factor, his thoughts about the law (including his belief in a right to shoot intruders) affect the legal outcome much less than do the thoughts of the officials of his community about their legal duties when one neighbor shoots another. The legal tradition that all persons are presumed to know the law reflects this lack of concern with a subject's thoughts about the law.

Officials of a legal system divide into four major groupings—judicial, enforcement, administrative, and ministerial—with the following functions and ways of doing their legal thinking:

- Judicial—Judges are entrusted with interpreting the law. They think about what the law means in various factual contexts.
- Enforcement—Because universal law enforcement would bring society to a halt (working by the book is an effective substitute for striking), officials are needed to decide which criminal and regulatory laws will be enforced against whom. While police officers and prosecutors need some notion of the meaning of law, their main concern is with weighing various factual

situations to achieve maximum social results from the cases they select to prosecute.

- Administrative—As social complexity grows, legislatures supplement traditional criminal and civil law with administrative law. Specialized government agencies are granted limited powers to function as legislatures, courts, and enforcement officials in making, interpreting, and enforcing rules in areas thought to require regulation. Thus, these administrators sometimes think as legislators, sometimes as judges, and sometimes as enforcement officials.
- Ministerial—Courts, administrative agencies, and other government offices need legions of clerks, with awesome powers but limited discretion, to see that the right papers are filed in the right places. While clerks usually do little thinking about the substance of law, legal procedures dominate their official lives.

Judges, enforcement officials, administrators, and clerks have duties, powers, and modes of legal thinking that vary widely, but they share characteristics that distinguish them from nonofficials. They all owe their first allegiance to a system rather than to an individual or a group. And, as organic parts of a system, they all are required to start their thinking from hypotheses that seem artificial to the rest of us: they must assume that the system exists and that the real-life events with which they deal and their official responses thereto have special meanings dictated by the system. They resemble game participants who, in order for there to be a game, must make assumptions about the game's existence and about the arcane meanings involved in its play.

Advisers

Subjects experience law directly, through their own persons and pocketbooks; and the working lives of officials are ordered by the law. In contrast, advisers in their professional capacity do not encounter law directly, but only vicariously as representatives of others. While officials as well as subjects have advisers and while not all advisers are lawyers, this section primarily concerns lawyers advising subjects. It explores three factors that influence how lawyers think: (1) they act as champions for subjects who need their loyalty; (2) these subjects are self-interested and result-oriented, whereas the officials with whom lawyers deal are supposedly disinterested purveyors of "blind" justice; and (3) lawyers must mediate between the practical goals of their clients and the formal rules that control officials.

As advisers, lawyers act not for themselves (like subjects) nor as organic parts of a legal system (like officials)—instead, they act as agents or fiduciaries for others. This removed position enables advisers to be more objective than subjects and less rule-bound than officials, but it also makes advisers less free to act on their own values and judgments. They cannot give their first allegiance either to their own consciences or to the system because they owe this allegiance to the interests that have been entrusted to them by their clients. While lawyers are called "officers of the court" and assume some official responsibilities to the system, these responsibilities usually yield when they conflict with the interests of a client. Judges are supposed to approach meaning free of bias; advisers are under a duty to look for meaning that will favor their clients. (This duty to look for favorable meanings is stronger when representing a client in litigation than when helping a client plan for the future.)

Advisers seek not the best nor most logical meanings of legal norms and events but rather the meanings that will most effectively serve their clients; they then work to justify these meanings as the best and most logical. For example, the lawyer for A, the man who shot and killed a person he thought was trying to break into his house, must strive to make plausible an interpretation of the law of homicide that justifies or excuses killing by one who thinks that his home is being invaded. The lawyer must make this effort—even if he deplores what A did and believes that the law will be worse and less logical if it justifies or excuses killings like A's—because A is entitled to the assistance of a lawyer who puts A's interest ahead of the lawyer's own conscience or convictions about social welfare.

To understand the position of advisers, differences between the positions of subjects and officials need to be re-emphasized. For subjects, law is like the weather and the economy: it is simply another inescapable fact that can affect their lives for good or ill. For officials, law has a different inescapability because they see it not as a fact but as a formal hypothesis without which their work would be nonsensical. Furthermore, subjects and officials use the law for different purposes. Subjects employ it to accomplish their own goals, whereas officials are supposed to have as their sole goal the survival, coherence, and perfection of the system of which they are a part. Thus, when subject and official confront one another they often seem to speak different languages.

Imagine the following dialogue between S and O, S being a subject who wants to incorporate herself because she has heard that incorporation is a way to avoid personal liability, and O being an official in the office of the Secretary of State in S's state:

> *S:* I was told that this is the place to get incorporated.
>
> *O:* That's right. You file articles of incorporation with me and pay a fee, and if your papers are in order, I will accept them and your business will be incorporated.
>
> *S:* You misunderstand me. I just want to incorporate myself so people can't sue me.
>
> *O:* But that's ridiculous! You can't just turn yourself into a corporation. If you could do that, everyone would want to do it, and pretty soon there would be nobody left.
>
> *S:* Oh.

To mediate this apparent impasse, a lawyer (L) would advise S that, while she cannot simply incorporate herself, she can form a corporation to carry on many of the activities likely to create liabilities—like selling services and other commodities, or operating a nonprofit enterprise—if she provides the corporation with enough assets to meet its probable liabilities. L would offer to prepare the kind of papers that would accomplish what S wants to do and that O would accept, for L realizes that O reacted as he did because what S asked for did not fit the legal norms under which O works. O understands what the law requires, but he has little incentive to understand S's goals or to help her achieve them because O does not see such help as part of his job. S, however, neither understands nor cares what the law requires—rather, she has goals that she has trouble expressing. L is able to help S because L shares O's understanding of the legal norms; because L can assume S's goals as his own; and because L can interpret the norms under which O works and articulate S's goals so that these norms and goals fit together.

A caveat is needed concerning L's attitudes about norms and goals. While it is essential that advisers know about the norms that govern officials, it is also essential that they experience them differently from how officials do. They must not accept, in the unquestioning way of most officials, the meanings of the legal system, for advisers need to be open to new meanings that might help their clients. At the same time, while advisers should temporarily take on the goals that motivate subjects, they should experience these goals differently from how subjects do. They should not permit goals to take the place of norms, as often happens in the minds of subjects—advisers need to be open to new legal meanings, but they should not fall into the trap of thinking (and they should not encourage their clients to think) that anything can be made legal by a clever lawyer.

Legislators

Subjects, officials, and advisers usually can be identified with little trouble. Legislators are harder to categorize because they include not only those who enact legislation as members of legislative bodies but also a variety of other people who sometimes make law in less formal ways—officials (such as judges and administrators) and even subjects. And, with officials, it is not always easy to be sure whether they are making new law or following existing law.

This section starts with formal legislators who enact new law, for themselves and the rest of us (including judges) who experience law that has already been made by someone else. Then it looks at those who create new law informally as a by-product of making other decisions. And finally, it compares the discretion of informal lawmakers and that of those who are simply being subjects of or officials for existing law. Just as officials and advisers are also subjects in their private lives, so all lawmakers, formal and informal, also experience law as its subjects. But depending on the capacities in which we act, our points of view will be quite different.

Lawmaking in its clearest form is enactment by a legislative body of a new legal rule for future application. Focus on future rather than existing law is a distinguishing characteristic of the legislative perspective: subjects, officials, and advisers think mainly about laws that have already come into being. In deciding whether to adopt a new law, formal legislators are constrained only by constitutional and statutory limitations on their legislative powers. Unlike subjects, officials, and advisers, legislators are not required to take into account any existing laws other than those limiting their own powers. And, while elected legislators may—and most do—take into account the interests and attitudes of their constituents, they do so by choice, not as a matter of legal duty. Within their powers, and apart from the exigencies of re-election, legislators are free to follow their own consciences and their own conceptions of the general welfare. Furthermore, while those who enforce and interpret the law both are controlled by legal standards and may be reviewed by higher authorities, legislators have almost complete discretion to do as they please: they use their own standards in enacting new laws and, subject to executive veto power and judicial check on whether they have acted within their legislative powers, these enactments are not reviewable. The legislative perspective thus can be likened to that of artists and authors who are free to put in or take out of their creations what they think best.

In addition to formal lawmaking by enactment, a less formal kind of lawmaking is performed by people (most notably judges and administrators) who are not members of legislatures. In the U.S. legal system, this freedom to do informal lawmaking, inevitable though it is, conflicts with the separation-of-powers concept thought to be prescribed in the Constitution: the concept that the legislative branch makes law, the executive branch enforces it, and the judicial branch interprets it. This conflict between freedom and structure creates one of the central tensions in legal thinking, developed further in Chapter 4. For now, it suffices to emphasize the important but often elusive differences between formal legislators who enact statutes and informal legislators who create law through other means.

One difference is functional: formal legislators write the texts of new laws of general application, while informal legislators only add new meanings to and applications of existing general laws. For example, some judicial interpretations (particularly those of the Supreme Court) take on the aura of holy writ, but they nevertheless are not authoritative texts, as constitutions and statutes are. In 1954 the Supreme Court drastically changed its 1896 interpretation of the words in the Fourteenth Amendment about "equal protection of law" as they apply to racial segregation in public facilities. But the words themselves will remain the same until they are changed by another constitutional amendment. Another example: although officials who create marriages and corporations and subjects who create contracts and property transfers are making new law in the sense that they are conjuring up new legal entities and relationships, they are not writing new legal rules of general application. Rather, a corporate charter or a contract is a kind of authoritative text, but one that makes a new legal norm only for the parties involved.

Another difference between formal and informal lawmakers is the extent of their discretion: the former may exercise broad discretion on policy matters in enacting new laws, but the discretion of the latter is bounded by pre-existing rules and principles, is ordinarily directed at specific situations, and is less open to policy arguments. Consider judges as an example. They are not supposed to defy or ignore the rules and principles found in statutes; they are generally limited to deciding only the cases before them; and, while they sometimes hear and use policy arguments, they do so more diffidently than do legislators, frequently by trying to transform policy considerations into matters of principle.

A third difference, akin to that of discretion, is the difference in perspective between formal and informal lawmakers. This difference can be likened to that between those who decide what the rules of a game shall be and those who officiate at a specific contest. The rule-making officials of organized baseball might appropriately consider whether the number of strikes allowed a batter should be increased from three to four, but it would be out of place for an umpire to hear argument on this issue during a game. However, if the norm in question is less clear-cut—say, if it attempts to define a "called" strike—the umpire can expect to hear plenty of argument about its application.

While the discretion of an informal lawmaker is narrower than that of a member of a legislature, it is broader than that of a subject or official who is not making but simply is following or experiencing the law. Although baseball umpires have no discretion about allowing more than three strikes, they have considerable discretion in defining what a strike is—a matter on which the players have no discretion at all. Similarly, subjects have choices about their contractual obligations that they do not have about their duties to refrain from committing crimes and from injuring other people, since courts do not enjoin violations of most contracts but do enjoin commission of most crimes and torts. And judges and administrators feel freer to entertain policy arguments about changing judicial or administrative rules than about departing from statutes. Thus, it seems that all participants in a legal system have some situations in which they can elect to become informal lawmakers by making new law, and other situations in which they necessarily are law experiencers since the existing law clearly tells them what they should do. And when people function as the makers, formal or informal, of new law they are in a position to think differently—with the potential of more autonomy, power, and concern for the future—than they are when they simply experience law that has already been put in place by someone else.

Legal Scholars

For the subjects, officials, advisers, and legislators considered thus far, perspectives and goals are fixed by their positions and functions within a legal system. Now we move outside the legal system to legal scholars who teach or write about it.

As suggested earlier, lines between advisers, officials, and legal scholars are blurred in the United States by the ease with which law-trained people can move about among law practice, government work, and law teaching and writing. Nevertheless, those who make these moves are aware that their perspectives and priorities change. An attraction of academic law, counterbalancing its lesser financial rewards, is a freer, more autonomous position from which to think. For a legal scholar, the constraints imposed by a legal system are exchanged for those imposed by the obligation to acquire and pass on an understanding of that system (and of legal systems in general). The kind of thinking needed for teaching and writing is different from that for solving the "given" problems of law practice—sufficiently different that those past the age of forty often are not encouraged to switch from law practice to teaching.

For example, corporation law teachers lack the built-in focus for their thinking that practicing corporation lawyers derive from the aspirations and adversities of a particular corporation. Rather, teachers are expected to bring sense and order, for themselves and their students, to the entire special world of corporations. Although teachers often use hypothetical problems to simulate some of the givens of practice, their goal is not to solve these imagined problems—instead, they strive to acquire and impart an understanding of how corporations work that will enable a student to deal with a variety of unidentified problems that are yet to happen.

Teaching and writing are both done from outside the arena of a legal system, but their perspectives are not identical. Teachers are less detached from the system, both because of the audiences they address and because of what they say to them. They address students who for the most part are preparing to become active participants in the legal system and thus want to know how the system works—and usually not much else. They meet students in daily, face-to-face encounters and fashion much of their teaching on the responses they are able to arouse. In contrast, writers can choose both their audiences and their messages. They can write for teachers, legislators, judges, lawyers, law students, other writers, various segments of the public—and even for subjects in general. And they are not confined to describing the legal system as it is: they are freer than teachers to explore new ways of thinking about and improving that system. However, lacking the immediate feedback provided by student response, a writer's thinking depends more on self-generated and self-tested ideas. And because a book or article is less ephemeral than a classroom lecture or discussion, a writer can be held to stricter standards of precision and rigor.

Nevertheless, teachers and writers have some common targets for thinking about law (as distinguished from the on-the-job thinking done in a legal system by its subjects, officials, advisers, and legislators). These targets include the law's coherence, its improvement, and (most fundamentally) its identity. In other words, academic legal thinking can seek legal clarity, social good, and philosophical understanding. Law teaching usually concentrates on conveying a coherent picture of how a segment (say, that relating to procedure, crimes, torts, contracts, or property) of the legal system works; and much legal writing is aimed at helping law teachers and others put together the components of these segments of the law. Furthermore, social good is a common goal of both parts of legal scholarship: some attention in teaching, and more in writing, is given to how legislatures, judges, and other officials might change existing laws to improve how they fit together or how they serve society. And the philosophical problems of whether and, if so, how, law is to be identified and given meaning pervades legal scholarship—both in classrooms and in commentaries. While thinkers from other perspectives may seek to make the law coherent, good, and understandable, they seldom can do so with the objectivity of legal scholars.

The points of view discussed in this chapter emphasize the diversity in legal thinking. In contrast, the norms and facts that provide the materials for legal thinking (to be discussed in Chapter 2) emphasize a sameness in legal thinking.

Chapter Two

MATERIALS FOR LEGAL THINKING

The materials for legal thinking divide into two basic categories, normative and factual. Normative materials include the rules, principles, and methods we call legal, along with moral norms derived from attitudes, obligations, and ideals. Factual materials—encompassing any materials employed that are not normative—are even more diverse. They include both objective data about events and their circumstances and subjective judgments about the consequences of applying (or not applying) legal norms to events.

A normative statement (a norm) says what ought to happen, in contrast with a factual statement that attempts to say what is, has been, or is likely to be. While the norm-fact difference frequently is ignored on the surface of ordinary discourse, it usually is respected in what is meant and understood. (For example, if a man says to his wife, "You ought to go to the bank today," she will probably interpret the message as a factual one—"We need cash"—even though it employs the normative word *ought*. But if he adds, "After all, you are my wife," she will perceive that he is telling her what she ought to do.)

To explain what is meant when a statement is called normative, resort is often made to saying it is nonfactual, reflecting an assumption that the universe of legal thinking is divided into two realms, factual and normative. Despite the seeming mystery of norms, they are discussed here before facts. This is done both because they are more distinctive to legal thinking and because it is hard even to start talking about the factual part of legal thinking until that part is defined—in the related senses of being limited and of being given meaning—by the normative part. However, as I hope will become apparent, the process of definition works both ways between norms and facts.

The materials for legal thinking are in some ways more fundamental than its points of view. While most modern legal systems provide a variety of perspectives for legal thinking, systems can be imagined—such as the one depicted in the Old Testament—with only a mass of subjects and a few officials who enforce a received and seemingly unchangeable body of laws. But even in such an apparently uncomplicated system, there would be a difference between normative and factual materials, between statements about what ought to be (you ought to pay your taxes) and statements about what is (you did not pay your taxes). And in any legal system, rudimentary or developed, the norm-fact separation is less vivid for subjects than for officials. Subjects, seeing the law as just another fact of life, can lump death and taxes together as the inexorables; tax officials, however, owe their jobs to the differences in the certainty of one's death and of the payment of one's taxes.

Points of view for legal thinking result from the various roles that people perform in a legal system. Materials for legal thinking are in part determined by the roles of the thinkers, but the classification of these materials is along different lines. Compared with the categories of perspective examined in Chapter 1, the division between normative statements and factual statements is less dependent on the structure of a particular system. When the norm-fact dichotomy is questioned by those who see norms as illusions, the questioning is usually done about norms in general rather than about the norms of a particular system. And all people called on to make legal choices or decisions, including those who see themselves as simply predicting what officials in fact will do, need some method—even though they may shrink from calling their method a normative rule—of identifying which facts, out of the welter of factual materials available, should be taken into account.

Normative Materials

In an analysis of normative materials for legal thinking, a good place to start is with the question: Who is telling whom to do what? The answer will identify the authoritative voice, the person addressed, and the content of the utterance. Norms become legal norms, as the term is used here, when they are backed by the authority of a government and addressed to subjects, officials, or legislators. With a moral norm, the identity of its backing is less determinate. A moral norm may be a religious tradition, a social custom, a professional code, or an ideal about human behavior that is claimed to transcend particular religions, societies, and other groupings. Those to whom such moral norms are addressed may also be less determinant, because with moral norms we have more freedom of choice whether to listen than we have with legal norms. And when a moral norm derives from individual conscience, the situation is still different, because the one doing the telling and the one being told are the same.

Whether dictated by the law or by morals, normative content seems to vary most significantly in terms of its importance and its specificity. Norms may be trivial traffic regulations, rules of etiquette, or personal quirks; or they may be fundamental constitutional limits on governmental power, religious and moral imperatives, and "sticking points" beyond which our consciences will not let us go. And norms may be specific, like a speed limit of fifty-five miles per hour, or they may express an imprecise aspiration, such as the admonition of tort law that we treat one another with "due care."

Legal norms: Rules, principles, methods

The prime normative materials for legal thinking are the legal rules currently being enforced by governments having or likely to have power over the thinker. Rules of other times and other governments, lacking power to punish the thinker, are "mere" facts—of possible historical or anthropological interest, but not of necessary concern in planning one's conduct. While it may seem that the unenforced rules of one's own governments resemble foreign or repealed rules in that it seems safe to disregard them, the possibility always exists that they will come to life and that disregarding them will cease to be safe.

We tend to see legal rules as addressed to subjects and enforced at the initiative of officials. Actually, the situation is often the reverse. Rules for identifying, changing, and adjudicating the law—sometimes called secondary rules to distinguish them from primary rules about the conduct of subjects and enforcement officials—are by their terms addressed to legislators and judicial officials. And, because the enforcement of all legal rules, primary and secondary, ultimately depends on government action, some legal theorists claim that all legal rules are, in effect, addressed to officials rather than to subjects. Outside the areas of criminal and regulatory laws, however, actual initiatives to put rules in motion are more typically provided by subjects than by officials. For example, unless the party injured by a tort or contract violation takes the initiative, the legal system ordinarily will do nothing about it. And, as noted in Chapter 1, ordinary citizens themselves create new legal rules by their contracts, conveyances, incorporations, marriages, and the like.

Compared with legal rules, legal principles tend to be less specific, more basic, and more likely to be directed to governments. For example, the legal norm that sets a speed limit of fifty-five miles per hour—with its specificity, comparative triviality, and address to subjects—seems quite clearly a rule. In contrast, our constitutional norms of due process and equal protection need laborious interpretation and application to be made concrete, are hardly trivial, and are addressed to governments rather than to subjects—although subjects need to take them into account in their legal thinking. Of course, important legal principles are addressed to subjects rather than to governments, such as the principles that admonish use of due care and fairness in conduct that affects others. And, while the legal rules about killing seem basic but specific, their actual lack of specificity introduced by exceptions for killings that are "justifiable" (because they are compelled by official duty or self-defense) or "excusable" (because they result from innocent accident or impaired capacity) and by mitigations for lack of malice (as when killings are provoked or unintentional) makes these seemingly clear-cut rules take on the open-endedness of principles.

Legal methods often resemble rules in that they are quite specific, and, compared with principles, they are even more preponderantly directed to officials but are somewhat less basic and more subject to change. Legal methods are normative in being officially prescribed ways to act, dictated by a higher authority or a statute. Those who argue that legal rules are largely illusory—or, at best, a matter of interpretation—assert that legal thinking is predominantly about methods rather than about rules, that it primarily involves making predictions about how judges and other officials are likely to react to given events. Others accept the importance of knowing how controversies are resolved, particularly in areas in which hard-edged rules are inappropriate, but assert that the method used is the product of some more general, underlying rule or principle.

An example of replacement of a specific legal rule by a legal method based on a more general rule or principle is provided in the area called "conflict of laws": when a judge chooses whether to use a rule of State X or State Y to determine a particular issue. Quite specific rules formulated to control this choice—say, that a tort issue, where A has injured B, should be governed by the law of the place of the tort—often have proved unworkable or productive of irrational results. Is the place of the tort the place where A acted or failed to act, or is it the place where B was injured? If A and B both live in State X but A happens to injure B in State Y, does it make sense to apply Y's law? Questions like these have led many states to discard the old choice-of-law rules in favor of a method in which the judge analyzes the respective interests of States X and Y in the issue to be decided. Judges have ceased to be bound by a rule; however, they still are not free simply to do as they please, because they still are required to follow a method.

New methods may also give new effects to rules and principles without changing their formal content. Before the mid-1930s, the method used by the Supreme Court to weigh compliance with the constitutional requirement that governments accord subjects due process included judicial review of the substantive reasonableness of the governmental action. In the late 1930s, the Supreme Court changed its method in due process cases, particularly those involving economic interests of subjects, to limit its inquiry to the fairness of procedures followed by government agencies, thereby averting collision with the legislative and executive branches but keeping intact the words of the Constitution. And after the Supreme Court changed its method for assessing due process, the new method became normative for other officials.

Moral norms: Attitudes, obligations, ideals

Legal rules, principles, and methods do not account for all the normative materials used in legal thinking: a residuum remains that will be lumped here under the heading of moral norms. The relationship between law and morals—the subject of Chapter 5—has long perplexed legal philosophers and has engendered a basic disagreement between the two legal theories, labeled as natural law and legal positivism. Proponents of natural law in its most rigorous form claim that immoral law is not law at all. Positivists reply that pedigree, not content, identifies valid law. At this point, I will sidestep this quarrel by simply saying that even though moral content is probably not a necessary condition to a norm's status as law, moral norms are needed to give meaning to legal norms and often determine whether legal norms will be applied in concrete situations. My aim here is to identify these moral norms and briefly to illustrate how they may fit into legal thinking.

Two common characteristics shared by moral norms are first, that unlike legal norms, they do not owe their existence to law, and second, that like legal norms, they provide standards for human behavior. Differences among moral norms arise from their sources: community attitudes, obligations imposed by positions and individual consciences, and ideals of justice and fairness. Here the following terms will be used to designate various kinds of moral norms:

- Mores—Attitudes prevailing in particular communities (sometimes called social morality).
- Ethics—Obligations assumed in taking particular positions, such as professions and offices, public or private, and family and other intimate relationships.
- Conscience—Obligations assumed by particular people for themselves, for religious or nonreligious reasons.
- Justice and fairness—Ideals of right and wrong for governments in governing and individuals in dealing with others. Such ideals may help form the attitudes and obligations described above.

While these materials all have normative content, their susceptibility to factual proof varies: attitudes that "prevail" are more provable than obligations that are "assumed" (yet both seem to be "positive"); and, to the extent that ideals are provable, it would seem to be by argument, not by evidence (since ideals tend to be "speculative").

An example of resort to moral norms to give meaning to legal norms is provided by the law of negligence. In assessing what constitutes due care in a specific situation for an ordinary person, the standard of care of a "reasonably prudent" person is used, drawing on the positive morality of the community. The issue of due care is usually left to the jury, because the jury is supposed to speak for the community. Less successfully, mores of the community have also been used to identify what kinds of expression are "obscene" and thus not subject to constitutional protection.

In assessing the behavior of people in positions of trust (lawyers, doctors, pastors, accountants, bankers, corporate executives, government officials), a relatively strict, specialized, idealistic ethic customarily is invoked to measure whether they have met the obligations of care and loyalty that the law assigns to them as a consequence of their assuming their positions. Questions about ethical obligations are less likely to be left to juries than are questions about the mores of a community.

While judges are empowered by the Uniform Commercial Code to refuse to enforce "unconscionable" bargains, and conduct of police officers that "shocks the conscience" has been held to violate due process of law, the individual consciences of judges deciding cases and of lawyers advising clients may not be trustworthy guides in interpreting and applying legal norms, since judges and lawyers generally are not supposed to impose their own consciences on others. However, for subjects planning their own conduct and for legislators considering new laws, use of their consciences is not only permitted but also encouraged. And the individual consciences of legal scholars are the main source of standards for the integrity of their own legal thinking as they try to explain to others how the law works.

Ideals of justice, which set standards for how government officials should treat subjects, are the foundations of much of our constitutional law; and ideals of fairness, which set standards for how subjects should treat one another, pervade much of our private law. Justice and fairness are sometimes measured by moral standards that seem, like positive law, to have ascertainable sources: the mores of a particular community, the ethics of particular positions, or the consciences of particular people. However, judges and other officials often look beyond such "positive" mores, ethics, and consciences to find that a particular behavior is unjust or unfair. In school desegregation cases, the Supreme Court went beyond community attitudes in many parts of the country. And judicial and administrative rulings about the obligations of corporate insiders to refrain from using inside information to profit from buying or selling their corporations' securities are examples of where judges have gone beyond the demand of an existing business ethic and of individual consciences.

Factual Materials

This section first examines the relatively objective factual materials for legal thinking provided by thinkers' perceptions of and assumptions about external events and circumstances. Then it considers the more subjective, but still essentially factual, materials provided by thinkers' judgments about what is prudent in light of the probable consequences to relevant interests and values—judgments that provide much of the fact side of the norm-fact tension described in Chapter 6.

Events and circumstances

Data that can be perceived or assumed by a legal thinker include the particulars of events that precipitate situational legal problems (as will be discussed in Chapter 3) and more general circumstances that may or may not surround events, depending on whether the problem is situational or abstract. The legal thinking of subjects and officials and their advisers is largely situational and thus depends on events. In contrast, the objective factual materials for legislators and legal scholars tend to be circumstances rather than events. Setting limits of relevancy on how far to go in probes for more and more details about events and in outreachs for broader and broader historical, economic, political, and psychological data about circumstances is one of the challenges of legal thinking.

For an example of a legal problem in which the relevant facts are mainly background circumstances, consider the following: When corporate officers and directors voluntarily undertake programs for the public good (say, locating a plant in a depressed area to be staffed by hard-core unemployed) that cannot be directly justified on a profit basis, are the officers and directors illegally "wasting" their corporation's assets, or are they making a legitimate exercise of their "business judgment"?

Objective factual materials, whether about events or circumstances, differ from the prudential judgments discussed later in that events and circumstances can be witnessed or postulated and are not necessarily the products of the thinker's judgments. The plant location problem would, of course, involve both objective data and subjective judgments.

Lawsuits can involve many kinds of factual materials—about events, circumstances, and judgments—but they are usually triggered by specific events. Foreground facts about events are provided by participants, witnesses, and physical evidence (e.g., documents, tapes, fingerprints, blood-stained garments). Background circumstances require going further afield to such sources as experts, surveys, and published data. Because foreground facts usually work more powerfully on the minds of judges and juries, the rules of evidence regarding the proof and testing by cross-examination of foreground facts are more stringent than are the comparable rules for background evidence; however, background evidence is more likely to be excluded as irrelevant.

For a situation in which subjects, advisers, and officials would concentrate on the particulars of the event, suppose that A and B collide in their automobiles. The legal rule in their state is that the one who did not use due care (who was negligent) should recompense the other, and if neither used due care, neither should recover. What facts are relevant to the issue of due care? Who ran into whom, how fast each was driving, whether either had been drinking, the time of day, and the state of their automobiles, the road, and the weather—all these factors may be relevant. Other facts might become relevant in combination with other circumstances, such as where they were going (if one is a doctor on the way to a hospital), what they were wearing (if one is wearing dark glasses at night), or the color of their cars (if one car was a color that is hard to see at the time of day of the collision). And there are infinite other factual details—such as the drivers' hair colors, political affiliations, or sexual preferences—that could be relevant only in combination with very unusual other circumstances.

Suppose that, instead of a controversy about whether either of these parties was negligent, the legal problem at hand is whether the contributory negligence rule (that nobody recovers if both parties are negligent) should be changed to allocate the cost of an accident on the basis of "comparative negligence" (that if A's negligence constituted 25 percent of the cause of the accident and B's 75 percent, B should bear 75 percent of A's damage). Now, relevant facts move from specific details about an event to quite general background considerations. The latter might include the history of the contributory negligence rule, the economics of permitting more recoveries, the policies about rewarding those at fault and about requiring judges and juries to quantify negligence, and the respective psychological impacts of the contributory and comparative negligence rules. Thus, the legal thinking "about facts" of a subject, adviser, or judge involved in a particular case is usually quite different from that of a legislator or a legal scholar debating a change in the law. Of course, if an effort is made to change the law by the decision in a particular case—as has been done on occasion with the change from contributory to comparative negligence—adviser and judge will be thinking about both the details of an event and the general considerations mentioned above. The difficulty in combining these different ways of thinking about facts helps explain why judicial legislation is discouraged.

Subject and adviser also go further afield than the details of events when planning a subject's course of action in the light of requirements of specific legal norms. Suppose that C, a client who operates a trucking service on a highway with a speed limit of fifty miles per hour, asks L, C's lawyer, how much above the speed limit, if at all, C should instruct drivers to travel. Background circumstances that C and L might want to think about include economic consequences to C of travel at various speeds; practices of C's competitors; practices of the general public on this highway; practices of police officers and judges concerning speeding violations on this highway; probable costs, financial and otherwise, to C of arrests and convictions; and what constitutes a reasonable speed. While there are legal and ethical constraints on L's advising C to violate the law, C seems entitled to obtain from L his or her best prediction concerning what will happen if C chooses to violate the law. (Holmes's "bad man" approach—that the real state of the law is accurately reflected in a lawyer's advice to a bad man about what he cannot get away with—seems valid to this extent).

Note that this hypothetical situation involves most of the norms mentioned in the preceding section that may constrain a subject, his or her advisers, and officials who deal with the behavior: a rule precisely defining illegal behavior by subjects; a possible principle (or ideal) of reasonableness concerning the rule's application; a method followed by officials concerning its application; community mores regarding acceptable behavior; the business and professional ethics of clients, lawyers, and officials; and the dictates of their respective consciences. And facts relevant for subjects planning their own conduct—"Other people do it," or "The police do not enforce this law"—may be irrelevant for officials called on to act when a rule has been violated.

Background circumstances become materials for legal thinking in the following areas:

- Examination of history—In interpreting constitutions, statutes, and judicial decisions (whether the inquiry is about what the makers intended or, more fruitfully, about what the authoritative text has come to mean)
- Economic analysis—In situations involving valuation, determination of relevant markets, and effects thereon of marketing practices
- Political sensitivity—In constitutional and statutory controversies about the powers of governments and the rights of individuals
- Psychological inquiries—In the many occasions in which state of mind or mental capacity may be crucial

Even more generally, many kinds of legal problems—ranging, say, from debates about who owns the ocean floor to struggles for the custody of a child—require thinkers to deal from many perspectives with the background factual materials provided by the natural and social sciences.

Judgments about what is prudent

Thus far, I have assumed that the factual materials for legal thinking can be found "out there" in the objective world of highways and history and nature. This picture is incomplete because it leaves out materials that can be found only in the thinker's own mind: judgments about what is prudent in light of probable consequences to relevant interests and values. These judgments are not perceived or learned about or assumed, as are events and circumstances in the outside world; nor are these judgments susceptible to the same sort of proof in court. Rather, they are conclusions that one arrives at, prodded by norms, objective factual materials, and other judgments. And, having arrived at these conclusions, one tends to use them almost as though they themselves were objective facts as one proceeds on the way to other factual or normative judgments that may be still more abstract.

The most typical factual judgments of legal thinking seem to involve prudential concerns about (1) future events (consequences) that are likely to happen if other future events occur; (2) the utility of consequences (interests) for the welfare of given persons or groups (interest holders); and (3) the desires (values) of given persons or groups (value holders) concerning such consequences. Thus, the relationships are of one event to another; an event to an objective calculation about interest; and an event to a more subjective value. (These relationships are developed more fully in Chapter 6.) I use the term *value* to refer to what is desired, as a matter of fact, which may or may not be what is considered morally worthwhile.

Note that what serves one's interests may not serve one's values, and vice versa. For example, I may acknowledge that to buy a foreign car is in my economic interest and still prefer to buy a less efficient domestic product because I do not want to add to my country's unemployment and balance-of-payments problems. When I act on this value preference, I assume, perhaps erroneously, that what I do will effect the consequences I seek. This assumption illustrates how our value and interest judgments often depend on judgments about consequences. To give this illustration a legal interest, assume that I am an agent for someone else and thus under a legal duty not to sacrifice my principal's interest to promote my own patriotism. Or, for a legal value, assume that my government has placed an embargo on the purchase of foreign cars, which could add a desire to obey the law to my other reasons for not buying a foreign car.

Judgments about consequences, interests, and values are alike in generating conclusions about the factual meanings of events. But they use different standards to reach their conclusions: cause and effect, utility, and individual or group will. The process of thinking about consequences—in its pure state, which seldom exists—resembles the kind of thinking to which the natural sciences aspire, employing disinterested, value-free inquiry about the physical linkage between events. In contrast, thinking about interests and values focuses, not on a series of events, but persons or groups or institutions with needs—political, economic, and psychological—and with wills that organize what they want. The movement in these kinds of judgment seems to have three steps. First, there is the discovery of seemingly mindless, inexorable cause and effect: I find that I get burned when I put my hands in a fire to pull out chestnuts. Then there is a mindful, less inexorable, but still quite objective calculation of utility: I decide that I need the chestnuts less than

I need to avoid getting burned. And finally, there is an addition to my personal value system: I come to value unburned hands above roasted chestnuts—although I may still be willing to let other people risk their hands in pulling out chestnuts for me.

Consequences, interests, and values were involved in the illustrations used in discussing objective facts. In the highway collision between A and B, a central legal issue was who caused the accident. A party to an accident who does not physically cause it probably is not liable even if he or she acted carelessly. But it is less clear that a careless party who physically causes an accident (in the sense of but for what the careless party did there would have been no accident) is liable if the accident that happens could not have been foreseen because of its remoteness from the triggering act. This suggests that the law may temper physical causation with moral blameworthiness. Suppose that intoxicated driver A collides with sober driver B because an earthquake (called by the law an act of God because it is beyond human control) hurls their cars together. A will not be liable to B, because A's lack of due care did not cause the collision. Now suppose that A (no longer intoxicated) carelessly tips over a detour sign that startles a third driver, C, who drives off the road, and a large bull escapes from C's vehicle and charges into B. Despite the unbroken chain of physical causation—from A to the sign to C to the bull to B—it is doubtful whether A is liable to B, because A could no more foresee this sequence of events than he or she could an earthquake.

In deciding whether comparative negligence should replace contributory negligence, a legislature or court would take into account the various public and private interests (such as holding down litigation costs and insurance rates) and values (such as a desire to do what is fair) that are likely to be affected by such a change in the law. And the lawyer advising a client in the trucking business about how fast C's trucks should travel will make judgments about the consequences of compliance and noncompliance with the fifty-mile-per-hour speed limit, whereas the client will make judgments about the strength of his or her economic interest in being competitive, and about how he or she ranks the values that will be affected by obeying or not obeying the law.

While judgments about consequences, interests, and values permeate all thinking, the concern here is with how these judgments provide materials for legal thinking through the involvement of legal norms—an involvement that may take myriad forms. The very existence of legal norms is a circumstance that has factual consequences (someone may be sued or arrested) that affect individual and group interests (transaction of business may be more or less difficult; highways may be more or less safe) that may be ranked by individual and group values; and the law's existence itself sets the stage for individual and group values (people may obey the norm because they value being law abiding). Nevertheless, the factual consequences of a norm may lead to its disobedience because of their impact on interests or values. For example, public school desegregation has been resisted because its factual consequences have been seen as costly—in terms of taxes, educational quality, racial harmony, and individual freedom of association—and because of the low priority (value) that many people assign to eliminating racial barriers. A legal norm may also be a consequence of factual events, such as when two persons exchange promises, or when a new rule is promulgated by a legislature or a court.

In summary, prudential judgments about cause and effect, interest, and value combine with objective factual materials about events and circumstances and with legal and moral norms to make up the materials with which legal thinking is done from the several perspectives detailed in Chapter 1.

Chapter Three

PROBLEMS FOR LEGAL THINKING

Problems are questions or situations presenting uncertainties. Problems are legal problems when the uncertainties concern the identity, meaning, applicability, or application of legal norms. While, as the first two chapters demonstrated, legal thinking is not an exclusive preserve of lawyers nor are its materials confined to laws, its problems are limited to those involving legal norms—a circumstance that sets boundaries, albeit expansive ones, to legal thinking.

Legal problems can be classified by the points of view of those seeking to connect legal norms with other materials and by the kinds of other materials sought to be connected. However, although attention is paid to differences in points of view and materials, the organizing distinction for this chapter is between problems presented by abstract questions about the identity and meaning of legal norms and problems presented by specific situations that involve connecting legal norms to events. In other words, problems are classified according to whether a legal norm itself presents an uncertainty (Is this a legal norm? If so, what does it mean?) or helps resolve an uncertainty (What does an event mean in light of the norm?). For example, the seemingly certain legal status and meaning of a speed limit can become uncertain in the light of the conduct of subjects and officials who do not observe or enforce it. Is it really a legal norm, and does it really mean what it says? But, at the same time, the meaning of the conduct of subjects and officials can suddenly lose its ambiguity in the light of a legal speed limit when drivers decide to be law abiding or when officials decide to "do their duty" regarding specific speeding violations.

Problems of Identifying and Interpreting Legal Norms in the Abstract

This section first considers whether it is necessary or helpful to deal with abstract questions about the identity and meaning of legal norms in the absence of situational contexts. Having concluded that these questions are indeed real problems demanding legal thinking, I examine the threshold need to separate law from nonlaw: the assumption that, before one seeks meaning, one needs an authoritative text to interpret. Then the sources of legal meaning, both within the law (norms themselves and their prior applications) and outside the law (the purposes and legislative histories of norms, and events since their creation), are explored. Problems of using legal norms in situations are dealt with in the following section.

Can legal norms be identified and interpreted in the abstract?

Some question whether any norms, legal or otherwise, can be stated or understood except on a case-by-case basis. This attitude is encouraged by legal theorists who claim that rules, principles, and methods are not binding laws until they are applied by judges or other officials, and by proponents of situation ethics and other relativist moralities, who purport to free us from all abstract, before-the-fact duties with the assertion that what we ought to do always depends on circumstances—that is, on facts rather than norms. And it is true that lawyers and judges trained in the common law tradition tend to be less comfortable with abstract questions than with problems that come encased in situations ("I can not define *x* [say, obscenity], but I can tell an *x* when I see one."). And law teachers and writers, and even legislators, dealing with legal problems that are abstract (because they have no client to represent or case to decide), try to make their problems seem more concrete by copious recourse to hypothetical situations.

Notwithstanding widespread skepticism about and discomfort with abstract normative authority and meaning, it would seem that if we are to have normative systems, such as legal systems and games, the norms of the systems must be accorded some validity and meaning before, *and whether or not*, they are applied. A legally enacted speed limit of precisely fifty-five miles per hour and a baseball rule allowing a batter precisely three strikes speak authoritatively and clearly, apart from and before their applications. (That the speed limit is widely disregarded—while the three-strike rule is religiously obeyed—does not lessen its legality or cloud its meaning; rather, it indicates its relative unimportance to thc operation of the system, although impressive utilitarian arguments for its retention can be made in terms of safety and energy conservation.) And, while a legal rule against negligence and a football rule against unnecessary roughness have less precise meanings, even such open-textured norms provide standards by which conduct can be measured (in terms of reasonableness and necessity)—standards that have some meaning standing alone or connected with materials that are not purely situational. Most of us have some abstract, before-the-fact notions about how we want and think we are entitled to be treated by others, and these "golden rule" notions give some meaning to such imprecise standards as due care and unnecessary roughness.

Abstract legal problems that call for identifying and interpreting legal norms by connecting them with other norms and with nonsituational factual materials work toward the formulation of legal principles—that is, general formulas for determining validity and meaning—that facilitate application of the norms to future situations. A system that creates new, ad hoc norms for each situation is not only unjust, because subjects do not know what to expect, but also inefficient, because judges and other officials must start over again with each new case. (Witness the problems of the Supreme Court in dealing with capital punishment on a case-by-case basis.) Drafters of forward-looking documents—constitutions, statutes, contracts, wills, and corporate charters and resolutions—should be no more specific than they need to be, thereby minimizing the possibility that their work will become dated. And good legal education aims to pass on a grasp of a limited number of general principles and methods that will prepare students to deal with the myriad norms and situations that chance will bring their way. In contrast, situational legal problems work toward particularization of legal norms; the objective is to give as detailed instructions as possible for the case at hand, because even carefully formulated principles seldom can be applied automatically in specific situations. Thus, while legislators and other legal draftsmen, as well as legal scholars, work toward general principles of abstract validity and meaning, subjects and officials work toward particularized applications of norms in situations—and advisers need to be prepared to work in either direction.

Of course, legal norms often do acquire clearer validity and meaning through their application in specific situations. (For example, Delaware is attractive for incorporation in part because of the thoroughness, compared with most other states, with which its rules about corporations have been judicially applied, enabling lawyers to predict with relative confidence the responses of Delaware judges to new situations.) But subjects and officials (along with advisers and legal scholars) still are not free to do (or to advise or explain) as they please until norms have been applied. And even legislators, who are free to change the substance of most norms, may do so only within the limits on their authority set in advance by other norms in constitutions and statutes.

The ability of judges and other officials to change legal norms in the application process—as the Supreme Court has done with the constitutional norm forbidding a state to "deny to any person within its jurisdiction the equal protection of its laws"—is not inconsistent with norms having legal status and meaning before as well as after they are applied in situations. The Fourteenth Amendment words about equal protection put some legal constraint on state governments when they became part of the constitution in 1868. Between 1896 (*Plessy* v. *Ferguson*) and 1954 (*Brown* v. *Board of Education*), the Supreme Court interpreted this constraint as not forbidding public facilities for different races that were "separate but equal," an interpretation that still legally required that facilities be equal. And since 1954, the constraint has been interpreted to ban separate facilities, whether or not they are equal. This abstract norm, the product of both the words of the equal protection clause and their application, will continue to be authoritative until the words themselves are changed by constitutional amendment or are again reinterpreted by the Court, notwithstanding the possibility of new situations—like benign quotas and affirmative action programs—that raise new questions about what the norm means. And none of these situations is likely to bring on a major reinterpretation of equal protection comparable with that made in the *Brown* case, a shift that was decades in the making.

How is law separated from nonlaw?

A norm that is unconstitutional or otherwise beyond the legislative power of its maker, or regarding which prescribed procedures have not been completed, lacks status (validity) as a legal norm—although it still may figure in legal thinking as a fact or as a moral norm. The as-yet-unadopted Equal Rights Amendment to the Constitution is an example of such a norm. This subsection divides the problem of separating law from nonlaw into two levels: the systemic level (a system itself, its constitution, and its legislature) and the operational level (the apparatus and logic by which working legal norms are generated).

Systemic-level identification: The system itself, constitution, legislature

Questions about whether a legal system exists arise when an illegal force, internal or external, is used to change its legal norms or to detach part of the territory it governs. History abounds with conquests, revolutions, civil wars, and secessions that become legal only if they succeed. (The secession of the United States from Great Britain succeeded; that of the Confederate states from the United States did not.) Since the existence of an independent legal system is not referable to any "higher" law, it would seem to be a factual rather than a normative question. The existence of any normative system depends on a factually accepted (and not itself normative) hypothesis or assumption that is needed in order to have a normative system. For example, if various people are about to play a game, they must start by assuming that such a game exists.

Apart from crisis points of change that are resolved by the use of force from outside the system, we proceed as though legal systems (and games) exist and look to a hierarchy of norms within a particular system to identify what is and is not valid law. Assuming a decision to have a constitutional legal system, the hierarchy of norms underlying that decision is headed by constitutional norms, written or unwritten, which allocate and limit governmental powers within the system. Our federal constitution allocates powers among the legislative, executive, and judicial branches of the federal government and between the federal and state governments; and limits powers of governments, federal and state, against individuals. Law is supposed to be made by the legislative branch, enforced by the executive branch, and interpreted by the judicial branch. In 1803, early in our national history, the Supreme Court interpreted judicial power to include power to review legislation to determine its constitutionality—ironically, in a decision (*Marbury* v. *Madison*) whose immediate result was to invalidate a statute increasing judicial power. Thus, a body of largely judicially made rules and principles, called constitutional law, has developed to separate valid from invalid law.

While we have become accustomed to thinking of a legal system's formal lawmaker as a legislative body, through much of history sovereign legislative powers have been held by individual rulers (lawmaking power in Great Britain is still formally held by "the Queen in Parliament"). Whether the constitutional lawmaker be one person or many, the most impeccable pedigree possible for a legal norm is to be part of a statute adopted by a legislature acting within its constitutional powers and in accordance with its own procedures. Legal thinkers can fail to treat such a norm as valid law only by doing violence to the legal system and its constitution—although they have more leeway as to how they interpret and apply the norm. However, formal action by a legislature is not a necessary condition for legal validity, because many norms accorded respect as law are created by judges, other officials, and subjects. In short, legislative enactment tells us what is law, but it does not tell us what is not law.

Operational-level identification: Apparatus and logic

At the operational level, valid law is identified by the workings of a normative apparatus, with higher norms generating, validating, and becoming more concrete in lower norms. Under the constitution are statutes and norms made by judges, administrators, other officials, and subjects. Statutes authorize officials to make law, and these officials delegate some of their power to subordinates. At each level—legislature, higher officialdom (including administrative agencies), and lower officialdom—the lawmaking powers granted ordinarily are not necessarily wholly exercised. Grants of legislative powers are often quite broad because the grantees are expected to be able to make better laws when the times come to make them than the grantors can do in advance. As legislatures may exercise only a portion of their constitutional powers, similarly higher officials and agencies may exercise less than all of their statutory powers and lower officials may exercise less than all of their delegated powers. Thus, asking whether an official action is valid law usually raises questions of legal power in the agency sense—involving interpretations of statutes, rules, and delegations of authority—as well as questions of legal power in the constitutional sense. And constitutional questions, asking what can be authorized, are ordinarily reached by a court only after the court has decided that the official action being challenged is authorized by or under a statute.

It is at these subconstitutional levels of statutes, administrative rules, and delegations of authority that we find most of the working apparatus for identifying valid law. As this apparatus proliferates, lawyers find they must specialize and law schools find they can teach diminishing portions of the total valid law. Consequently, recent decades have seen a shift in legal education away from what this year's rules may require (which is likely to be out of date next year) toward imparting the systemic and operational processes that generate valid law, particularly the logic through which the validating apparatus works. This logic involves the deduction from general norms—concerning, for example, constitutional powers and rights, crimes and torts, property interests and contractual relationships—more specific norms for application by particular subjects and officials in legal situations. Although the main teaching tool continues to be the case method—the study of appellate decisions in actual cases—emphasis has shifted from extracting rules from these decisions to discerning the methods employed in dealing with legal situations at their various stages.

The norm-to-norm relationship by which specific norms (say, a contract between A and B) are derived from general norms (the law of contract) has been called imputation, because the general norm imputes (brings into the reckoning) the specific norm. This normative relationship is to be distinguished from the fact-to-fact relationship of causation in which one event (say, an explosion) causes another event (an injury to someone). Whether general norm *x* imputes specific norm *y* depends on their logical relationship in an artificial normative system; in contrast, whether fact *x* causes fact *y* depends on their physical relationship in nature; and the methods of testing and establishing these kinds of relationship are different. Imputation is mainly a question of logic and causation of evidence; although, of course, evidence (such as legislative records) and causation may aid imputation, and logic may be used in weighing evidence and determining probable cause.

The logic of imputation, of deriving specific norms from general norms, is an essential process for identifying valid law. The lower, more specific norm is both created and validated by its imputation from a higher, more general norm. For example, suppose that official O, directed by statute to grant incorporations for lawful purposes, is asked to incorporate a society to promote homosexuality. Whether O derives from the statute a specific norm for or against incorporation in this situation depends in part on O's logical deduction about how homosexuality relates to the standard of lawfulness that O is supposed to apply. And the legal validity of the norm that O imposes will depend in part on the logical validity of O's reasoning.

In deriving specific norm *y* from general norm *x*, the judge, other official, or subject is limited by the boundaries of *x* and is not free, as a legislature is free (subject only to constitutional and statutory limits on its powers), to fashion norms solely in light of their morality or expediency. For example, from the general constitutional norm of equal protection, as interpreted in the school desegregation cases, a more specific norm can be derived outlawing efforts by states or their subdivisions to establish racially segregated public recreational facilities. But because the general norm is limited to state action, thinkers are not free to derive therefrom a legal norm preventing a private club from having racial restrictions—even though they view such restrictions as immoral or impolitic affronts to human dignity. And whether Congress or a state legislature can enact a statute outlawing private racially restricted clubs raises questions of whether the general constitutional norms in the Bill of Rights impute more specific norms guaranteeing freedom to choose with whom one associates in the private parts of one's life, and whether membership in racially restricted clubs is a part of that freedom to associate.

How is abstract meaning sought within the law?

Most norms are stated by words in sentences, although they can be expressed wordlessly, as by the gestures of officials in contests, or by the shake of a parent's head. Search for the abstract meaning of a norm starts with attention to what it says. If the norm is a legal rule, the search begins within the law by examining the rule's own terms, its place in the legal system, and how it has been applied (or not applied) by subjects and officials. (A rule's purpose, legislative history, and background facts—clues to meaning from outside the law in the sense used here—are saved for later discussion, as are problems of applying meaning to new situations. However, because this subsection includes past applications of a rule as clues to meaning from inside the law, it is recognized that application of a rule both shapes and is shaped by the rule's meaning.)

The terms of a rule may be defined within the rule itself or according to procedures established by the rule. Alternatively, definitions may be left to be provided by other legal rules, by reference to moral and ethical standards, and by resort to factual categories, which are often definable by common sense and common usage. (For example, is an airplane a "motor vehicle"? Probably not.) As a consequence, many nonlegal normative and factual terms, including prosaic terms of ordinary discourse, when used in legal rules become, in effect, legal terms with special, conventional meanings for the purposes of the rules. To provide a feel for how terms used in legal rules both create and help resolve problems of abstract meaning, a sampling of rules about speeding, homicide, antitrust, securities regulation, and constitutional rights is offered.

Speeding

A rule establishing a speed limit of fifty-five miles per hour seems clear on its face as to what it says and means. It invests a normatively neutral speed with legal meaning. And it establishes a standard of conduct that needs little interpretation, because it can be precisely stated and measured, like the scoring and timing of a game. With a hard-edged rule of this sort, legal thinking might seem to concern the rule's application rather than its meaning. However, if the speed limit is seldom observed or enforced according to its terms and if police act only when some one drives at an "unreasonable" speed, the rule's abstract meaning becomes so dulled by disuse as to appear to be replaced by a soft "rule of reason"—although those who disregard the letter of the rule risk the sudden hardening of its meaning.

This speed limit would seem to convey a precise abstract meaning by which I can describe the legal meaning of my conduct on the highway: If I drive at fifty-six miles per hour, I am driving illegally. But the conduct of enforcing officials comes between my conduct and the rule and for all practical purposes changes the precise factual standard into an ambiguous standard of official discretion, under which a speed of fifty-six miles per hour would probably be permitted, but not a speed of eighty miles per hour. The very precision and hardness of a numerical standard create pressure to substitute a looser discretionary standard of reasonableness, because there are so many situations in which enforcement of the numerical standard can seem unreasonable to most subjects and officials.

Homicide

A rule outlawing murder may simply say that the crime of murder shall be punished by death or life imprisonment—assuming, with justification from legal history, that the word *murder* has an established legal meaning by which homicides may be classified as murder or not murder. But the abstract meaning of a murder rule obviously presents more complex problems, and needs to be stated more subjectively, than does a speeding rule. The legal standard for what is and is not murder cannot be stated in purely objective terms because it measures not quantifiable physical events (which may appear the same for innocent and culpable killings) but rather the mental states of people who kill.

To be ready for a situation in which A kills B, the law defines in advance several legal categories of killings (murder, manslaughter, and various kinds of culpable and nonculpable homicide), using subjective classifications about A's state of mind, such as premeditation, malice, intention, reckless abandon, and gross or ordinary negligence. The law also uses classifications about events preceding the killing that may mitigate A's culpability: B's provocation of A, which may negate A's premeditation and malice; A's acting in self-defense or by accident, which may excuse the killing; and A's acting in the line of duty as a police officer or soldier, which may justify the killing.

In short, the abstract meaning of murder gives special legal meanings to a killer's thoughts and circumstances. As a speed limit tells us with a number how we can avoid being speeders, the murder rule tells us with the concept of malice how we can avoid being murderers. While the meaning of murder uses subtler standards requiring more complex proofs than does the meaning of speeding, the clarity of murder's meaning remains less muddied by the discretion of enforcers. Murder is not a crime that most enforcers can overlook; and if a killing is considered "reasonable," it is usually not murder.

Antitrust

A federal statute, the Sherman Antitrust Act of 1890, outlaws contracts, combinations, and conspiracies in restraint of trade. However, because all business transactions restrain trade to the extent of taking the parties out of the market for the business transacted, in 1911 the Supreme Court construed the Sherman Act to outlaw only "unreasonable" restraints of trade. In effect, the Court added to the statute a word giving discretionary dimensions to its meaning.

Did the Supreme Court do to the Sherman Act what the police have done to speed limits? Not exactly. The Court said this statute is meaningless without a rule of reason; thus, Congress must have expected that the courts would use a rule of reason in interpreting its words. While speed limits may seem unreasonable, it is hard to argue that they are meaningless in the sense that subjects and officials do not know what they say. In addition, the Court added its own language to the words of the Sherman Act but did not substitute its own language for something else that was in the statute.

Over the years, the Sherman Act has become less discretionary because of judicial decisions defining unreasonable restraints in terms of anticompetitive motives and consequences and holding that some restraints—such as price fixing among competitors—are illegal per se and do not require further proof about motives or consequences. Thus, what is unreasonable in the antitrust context has acquired a special and quite specific legal meaning—like the meaning of murder—limiting the room for official discretion. And while, as with speeding, some leeway regarding antitrust compliance and enforcement remains, it is more "legitimate" leeway because the standard of reasonability, rather than being introduced informally by subjects and enforcement officers, has been written into the antitrust rule by the Supreme Court with the acquiescence of Congress.

Securities regulation

The federal Securities Act of 1933 requires that certain sales of securities be registered with the Securities and Exchange Commission (SEC) and defines the word *security* to include any stock. In refusing to apply the act to the sale by a nonprofit corporation of stock that entitled holders to rent apartments but that could not be sold for profit, the Supreme Court in 1975 said that such a transaction is not a security transaction "simply because the statutory definition of security includes the words 'any . . . stock'" (*United Housing Foundation, Inc.* v. *Forman*). In 1946 the Court created its own definition of a sale of security as involving "an investment of money in a common enterprise with profits to come solely from the efforts of others" (*SEC* v. *W. J. Howey Co.*). The act exempts from its registration requirement transactions "not involving any public offering" but does not define a public offering. After more than forty years of case-by-case application of these words, in 1974 the SEC adopted a rule that distributions to not more than thirty-five people qualify for the exemption if other conditions are met.

In trying to state abstract meanings for the statutory terms *security* and *public offering*, the Court and the SEC have worked in opposite directions, respectively loosening and tightening meaning. The Court said that the label "stock" is not sufficient to identify a security and that inquiry must be made into such factual matters as investment, common enterprise, and whether profits are "to come solely from the efforts of others." In contrast, the SEC said that a simple head count will go far in identifying what constitutes a public offering. But, in comparison with the subjective standards for murder and antitrust violations, both the Court and the SEC have provided quite objective standards for giving meaning to the Act's provisions.

Due process and equal protection

The Fourteenth Amendment reads in part: "No state shall . . . deprive any person of life, liberty, or property, without due process of law; nor deny any person within its jurisdiction the equal protection of the laws." This important text combines legal, discretionary, and factual terms.

Legal terms such as *state*, *person*, *property*, *process*, and *within its jurisdiction* are given meaning by other parts of the amendment, the Constitution as a whole, and the general body of legal norms of our legal system. For example, the clear meaning of the quoted sentence is that it restricts a state but not a subject. And the rest of the Constitution clearly indicates that *state* means one of the United States. But the text is less clear about the meaning of the word *person*; and this ambiguity has permitted the Supreme Court to interpret these guarantees as applying to corporate as well as to natural persons.

Words such as *liberty*, *due*, and *equal* leave much to judicial discretion. The meaning of equal protection has varied through history when it has been applied to racial classifications. In addition, there have been efforts to confine the meaning of due process to questions of procedure.

Words such as *deprive*, *life*, *deny*, and *protection* in the abstract seem normatively neutral, and thus in the realm of facts, although situations can be imagined in which they might raise legal or moral problems. For example, when does life begin and end?

The Fourteenth Amendment, made part of our law at the cost of a bloody civil war and kept an effective part by judicial independence and courage, well illustrates the place of abstract meaning in legal thinking. When subjects, officials, advisers, legislators, and legal scholars think about how the due process and equal protection clauses apply in specific situations, they cannot avoid making some preliminary assumptions about what these clauses say to the state governments about the limits of their powers.

Abstract meanings in these illustrations assume various shapes, ranging from the specifics of speed limits to the generalities of due process, from the timeless proscriptions against murder to the twentieth-century technicalities of antitrust and securities laws. But they all join to demonstrate that legal thinking about meaning begins within the law, with an authoritative text that usually has a history of prior applications by subjects and officials—although the search for meaning seldom can be completed without going outside the law.

How is abstract meaning sought outside the law?

In the preceding search for abstract meaning of a norm within the law, I have used an expansive, but not unlimited, concept of what is law. In addition to clearly legal sources (the terms and legal context of the norm itself, its prior applications, and meanings for its terms gleaned elsewhere in the legal system), I have included nonlegal materials that assume legal meanings by being incorporated into the norm through its language or interpretation. But I have taken care to read the norm as law—not as politics, sociology, or history (apart from the rule's own history revealed in its prior applications). My search has gone outside the four corners of a norm only when so directed by the text as authoritatively construed (as the Supreme Court construed the antitrust statute). Now I go further afield to matters clearly outside this definition of the law: to a norm's purpose, its legislative history, and events subsequent to its creation that temper its meaning. Now my concern is with evidence of a norm's abstract meaning provided by the why and how of its making and by what has happened outside the law since then.

Why was the norm made?

Strong-minded judges, like Holmes and Frankfurter, sometimes declare that a judge's job is to decide what a law means, not what its makers meant it to mean. They reject—with considerable justification in the light of the way much legislation is adopted—"legislative intent" as a legitimate consideration in judicial interpretation of legal norms. But these same judges often look outside the norm itself to the circumstances that led to its making. They distinguish subjective legislative intent about what legislators meant to say from objective legislative purpose about what they meant to do: what it was in the outside world that motivated them to legislate. These judges argue that the text itself is the best evidence of what the lawmakers meant to say, whereas the external circumstances leading to the legislation cannot be known simply by reading the text. And even when legislators employ a preamble that expressly explains a law's purpose, interpreters are not legally bound thereby, because preambles purport to state facts, not norms. The explanations of legislators of why they are legislating may, like legislative history, be interesting and even persuasive; but such explanations are still only some evidence of legislative purpose that may be rebutted by other, more objective evidence of the conditions causing the legislation.

The classic statement of the relation between a norm's meaning and the circumstances that caused it to be made is the "mischief" rule bequeathed to us in 1584 by Heydon's Case. There a court of English judges said that the way to construe a statute is to ask what the common law was before the statute, what the mischief was that the common law failed to curb, and what remedy the legislature has "appointed to cure the disease of the commonwealth," and then "to make such construction [of the statute] as shall suppress the mischief and advance the remedy."

The mischief rule at work can be seen in the construction given to federal statutes of 1933 and 1934 regulating the selling and buying of securities. The mischief that the common law failed to curb was insufficient disclosure of material information to those making investment decisions—a failure perceived as contributing to the stock market debacle of 1929. Meanings given to the securities statutes by the courts, the SEC, and the securities industry and bar have been strongly influenced by this congressional purpose, to which frequent references are still made.

The mischief rule was stated for and applies most smoothly to constructions of statutory rules that purport to fill gaps in the common law. However, its core idea—that new legal norms are made because of circumstances calling for legal controls—applies to legal norms generally, including constitutional provisions, common law rules, and legal norms generated by private transactions. For example:

- The purpose of the Fourteenth Amendment was to curb the mischief over which the Civil War was fought: assertion by some states of legal power to restrict individual rights and freedoms on the basis of race. (There may also have been a hidden agenda to protect business from state regulation; for many decades business enterprises benefited more than did individuals from the amendment.)
- The common law negligence rule, making one liable for injury to others from one's carelessness, developed because society is harmed if negligence is condoned and its victims are left to bear the burden of accidents. But the administrative costs and questionable fairness of making fault the test for liability have led to the development of rules governing accidents that de-emphasize fault, and these rules will in turn be interpreted in the light of this newly discovered mischief.
- Our private transactions may be with those close to us or with strangers. When we deal with those close to us, our purpose often is to avoid empty formalities; but when we deal with

strangers (or enemies), our purpose usually is to avoid vulnerability to being victimized. Thus, the meaning of a contract may be affected by whether or not it is made "at arm's length." For example, "technical" provisions about time of performance, giving notice, forfeiture, and the like may be construed differently.

How was the norm made?

Norms are meaningful only as parts of normative systems; and knowing the gap in the system that a new norm is supposed to fill tells us much about its meaning. But knowing a norm's legislative history—its evolution, often protracted and tortuous, through successive drafts and committees to the authoritative text—is of more limited assistance in fixing its legal meaning.

Textual histories of important documents, particularly of those that transmit a culture's religious and literary heritage (such as, in our culture, Homer, the Bible, and Shakespeare), do more for us than provide subjects for doctoral dissertations. Appreciation of a basic text is enhanced by what the reader knows about any earlier texts from which it may derive, about dating and authorship of different versions, and about changes that may have been introduced by compilers, translators, editors, and bowdlerizers. Similarly, judges, lawyers, and legal scholars, in searching for meanings of legal norms, sometimes resort to exhaustive analyses of legislative histories. (As an in-house legal joke goes: "If a law's legislative history is unclear, it may be necessary to consult the text.") It is questionable, however, whether knowing how a norm was enacted contributes to legal meaning in the same way that textual histories may contribute to religious or literary meaning, because legal meaning is not a problem of factual knowledge or belief or of aesthetic judgment.

In a stable legal system, authenticity of the sources of words used in legal norms is rarely an issue. Legal thinkers do not consult legal norms to learn facts, to instill or strengthen beliefs, to stimulate insights, to judge values, or to seek enjoyment. Their object is simply to learn the requirements and entitlements of the law. If a legal norm's final wording resulted from a change along the way, in committee or on the floor of the legislature, that may, like a preamble, influence a judge to give the finished product the meaning sought to be achieved by the change; he or she is not, however, legally bound to take that change into account in the same way he or she is bound to give attention to the text. What the lawmakers did, not what they intended to do, is the law. Thus, it seems that authoritative evidence of what a norm means is provided by legislative history only to the extent that this history helps to identify legislative purpose.

What has happened since the norm was made?

In searching outside the law for indications of what a legal norm means, we need to look not only back from its making to its purpose but also forward to what has happened since it was made. The original motivating mischief may have been displaced or overshadowed by new mischief. In 1927, when trains still seemed more important than automobiles, Justice Holmes (then 86), speaking for the Supreme Court, ruled that motorists crossing railroad tracks would need to dismount and look up and down the tracks in order not to be negligent (*Baltimore & Ohio R.R.* v. *Goodman*). Fortunately, in so ruling the Court was particularizing the meaning of a broader principle calling for reasonable conduct. Just seven years later, when it had become more apparent that the balance of trains and automobiles had shifted (and after Holmes had left the Court), the Court was able to find a new, more realistic meaning for due care in driving across railroad tracks (*Pokara* v. *Wabash Ry.*). This fragment of legal history shows the wisdom of keeping legal norms flexible. As conditions change, specific meanings that are written into norms are hard to change by interpretation; and, when specific meanings are imbedded in constitutions and statutes, they may be politically resistant to change by new legislation. Ambiguity has its virtues in wording legal norms.

In concluding this section on abstract meaning, I will resort yet again to the Fourteenth Amendment and the changes through which the principles of due process and equal protection have gone in this century. Factual and normative changes outside the law—in the workings of the economy and in moral attitudes, obligations, and ideals about what is tolerable and what is just—contributed powerfully to these changes in legal meaning. In 1900 substantive due process was a license for free enterprise to maximize profits and the separate-but-equal interpretation of equal protection a justification for racial segregation. Events appeared to call for increased public regulation of business in order to avert economic and ecological disasters, and also for increased protection of individuals against government action, in order to preserve freedoms and to correct and guard against discrimination. Judges responded to these extralegal changes with new legal meanings for the generalities of due process and equal protection. In the remainder of the century, if social disorder and scarcity of resources come to be perceived as central problems, or if advocates of minimal government prevail, the meanings of due process and equal protection are likely to undergo further change.

Problems of Applicability and Application of Legal Norms in Situations

So far in this chapter I have talked about questions: abstract, presituational questions regarding the identity and meaning of legal norms. Focusing on uncertainties about the law itself, these questions are like those put to lawyers and law teachers, and occasionally to judges and other officials, when they are asked what the law is, in isolation from occasions when it might be applied. In this section I will broaden the problems to encompass situations presenting uncertainties as to applicability and application of legal norms.

My pivotal distinction in this section is between conceptualizing situations to determine the normative applicability of norms to events and making choices or decisions whether to apply or not apply norms to events. First, I will consider how legal situations—intellectual constructs (concepts) made by legal thinkers from events, legal norms, and other factual and normative materials—are put together in order to reveal applicability (or lack of applicability) of norms to events. Then, I will consider how choices and decisions are made by subjects and officials about the actual application of applicable norms to events—choices by subjects to determine their own conduct, decisions by officials to determine how they will perform their jobs.

Although I will still be concerned here with questions of the identity and interpretation of legal norms, now "relevant" facts as well as "applicable" norms need to be selected and given meaning. And meanings of norms will no longer be purely abstract questions, uncomplicated by events and circumstances, but rather parts of situations that lead to the making of legal choices and decisions about the application of norms to events. Furthermore, problems of meaning and application seem to be bound together in a tantalizing chicken-and-egg relationship: the abstract meaning of a legal norm, shaped by any decisions about its application in prior situations, contributes to construction of the concept of this situation; in turn, the decision about the norm's application in this situation shapes its abstract meaning for the construction of future situations—and so on.

Conceptualizing legal situations about the applicability of norms to events

The objective facts of events—A strikes B and B dies; A and B accidentally collide in their automobiles; A and B talk business—provide starting points for constructing legal situations in preparation for making legal choices and decisions. But a legal situation is different from a raw physical event. It is a concept in the mind of a legal thinker about an event and its circumstances, and it combines the factual and normative materials that the thinker assembles to give the event legal meaning. The thinker constructs a concept of a legal situation by connecting factual materials about an event and its circumstances with possibly "applicable" legal norms—a process that may lead the thinker to think about other norms, legal or moral. This mental picture of the event in its factual and normative context becomes the legal situation.

Events that are purely ceremonial or formal (e.g., getting married or divorced, changing one's name, forming a corporation, signing or sealing a document, or swearing an oath) lack meaning apart from their legal consequences and thus connect more automatically with legal norms than do less formal, more ambiguous events with possible nonlegal meanings, as well as several possible legal meanings. For example, when A strikes B, it may be a friendly slap on the back, with physical and social but not legal consequences, or it may be an event with a variety of legal consequences, such as murder, manslaughter, or criminal or civil assault and battery; when A and B collide on the highway either or both parties may or may not have been negligent; and when A and B have a business talk, the result may be just conversation or a binding contract (and then the question becomes the meaning of the contract). An event implicating the negligence rule that one should use due care is doubly ambiguous, factually and normatively: the rule itself requires that the thinker assess, not only how much care the parties actually used (a factual finding) but also how much care is due in the situation (a normative conclusion).

The details of an event and its circumstances are not always knowable firsthand by legal thinkers (even by those who participate in the event) and often must be pieced together by making inferences from physical and testimonial evidence. Discovery of a situation's factual materials is a continuing process, governed by elaborate procedural rules for situations involving litigation. Law school teaching, with its concentration on appellate cases in which most of the facts are already established, understates the difficulty and importance of the fact-finding part of legal thinking. (Most practicing lawyers will tell you that they spend more time investigating facts than looking up law.) However, the law school emphasis on deriving the meanings of legal norms from decided cases and on connecting given events with legal norms is not as impractical as it may first appear. If a student can put together usable conceptions of the more basic legal norms, can recognize events to which these norms may apply, and can conceptualize legal situations that combine events, norms, and other arguably relevant materials, he or she has taken the necessary first steps toward dealing coherently with situational legal problems.

Situations, made specific by their events and legally meaningful by pertinent norms, can be expanded by describing the events so that additional norms are involved and by interpreting the norms so that still more norms and facts enter the picture. For example, suppose that a conversation resulting in what appears to be a contract takes place between an individual farmer, whose choice is between selling his crop now or risking not selling it at all, and a powerful corporation with a reputation for driving hard bargains. These background facts may bring into play the norm of contract law that a judge may decline to enforce a contract that he finds to be unconscionable, a norm that expands the situation beyond its normal legal boundaries.

The expandability of legal situations lessens as similar situations recur and legal thinkers are guided (and limited) by precedents in connecting events to norms and other materials. The interface is no longer between raw physical events and bare abstract norms, but between events with relevant features highlighted by comparisons with earlier events and norms with meanings made more concrete by applications in earlier situations. While the mental operation now is mainly one of comparing and contrasting situations, with diminished attention to the precise language of norms, the meanings of norms, albeit less abstract because of prior applications, still provide the criteria for distinguishing between situations.

In constructing concepts of legal situations that connect events to norms and possibly to other materials, legal thinkers initially are guided by logic: by the fit of events to the norms and prior events. But they may also need to think about other factors, such as the fairness to the parties and the utility to society of making the contemplated application of norm to event, and by the practical likelihood that such an application will be made. For example, consider whether an A-B event (intentional hitting, accidental colliding, or business talking) will be called, respectively, murder, negligence, or contract, if the A who hits and kills B is a police officer, or if the A who collides with B is a parent rushing a sick child to the hospital, or if the A who contracts with B has no feasible economic alternative. Are officials likely to consider it fair or useful in these situations to apply the legal norms of murder, negligence, or contract? But if these norms are not applied, what happens to the claims of B and of society? Is it fair to B or useful to society to say that all of the cost of the situation should fall upon B, just because A happens to be a police officer, or a distraught parent, or a person in a poor bargaining position?

These questions highlight the difference between a norm's potential for being applied and its actual application in a legal situation. It is usually the task of advisers to conceptualize a situation so that their clients, whether subjects or officials, have before them the factors that bear on this potential, including the demands of logic and consistency, considerations of fairness and utility, and probabilities of official action or inaction. But it is the subjects or officials themselves who choose or decide whether to obey or to enforce legal norms.

Making choices and decisions about the application of norms to events

Legal situations are conceptualized to prepare a legal system's subjects and officials to make choices and decisions about the application of norms to events. Subjects make choices about their own conduct to further their own interests and values (which may include being law-abiding citizens), and officials make and justify decisions about the conduct of others in order to carry out the powers and obligations of their offices (which do not, in a well-ordered legal system, recognize any choice about being law-abiding officials). The ideas of "choosing" by subjects and "deciding" by officials are used to convey the different qualities of what subjects and officials do regarding the application of norms to events. Chapter 6, which deals with the tension between norms and facts in applying norms to events, assumes that the norms are legally and morally applicable to the events—otherwise there would be no norm-fact tension. At this point, however, this assumption is not made; rather, it is recognized that a subject or official, particularly one unaided by a lawyer, may think about whether to obey or enforce a legal norm without first thinking about whether it is legally or morally applicable.

Advisers counsel subjects and officials about their choices and decisions but do not, as advisers, choose or decide for themselves. They often are the ones who develop the concepts of legal situations that define the issues to be resolved about the application of norms to events; and, when advising subjects or subordinate officials, they may predict how officials are likely to decide in the situations they have conceptualized. They are supposed to be experts about the abstract meanings of legal norms, the relevancy of facts to norms, and official thinking about the application of norms to facts: about how the decisional process moves from an event to a norm to form a situational concept, and then from this concept to an official decision as to whether the norm will actually govern the event.

Legislators and legal scholars do not face actual problems of application (or applicability) because their legal thinking does not depend on events; one does not need a precipitating event in the real world to legislate or teach or write. Legislators and legal scholars do, however, think about how legal situations are conceptualized, and about how legal choices and decisions are made and justified, because understanding these situations and determinations is essential both to making workable legal norms and to explaining how legal systems work. But this subsection focuses on subjects and officials, for they are the ones who actually make the choices and decisions about whether legal norms will be applied to events.

Subjects

When we, as subjects, choose whether to apply legal norms to events, we think about and for ourselves; and we are legally required to justify our conclusions only to ourselves, although we sometimes try to explain them to others. Our choices involve our own conduct, are influenced by our own respect for prudential authority and by our concern for our own interests and values, put at risk our own welfare, and are made on our own behalf—as principals, not as agents. And these legal choices are often so intermingled with the rest of the choices in our lives that they are difficult to isolate. For example, my choice to exceed a speed limit—made, perhaps, because I am in a hurry, or angry, or just thinking about something else—will not seem as legal to me as will, in his or her mind, the decision of the police officer who gives me a ticket. Our choices about being law abiding tend to get lost in the welter of our other concerns unless we make a conscious (and conscientious) effort to think about them.

Compared with officials making enforcement decisions, we as subjects make legal choices with relative freedom from the structures imposed by given events and norms. We are less constrained by events because we often can choose whether to commit the act that could precipitate a legal situation: whether to strike the blow that could become a crime or tort; whether to make or accept the offer that could become a contract. And, while we have a general duty to obey legal norms directed to subjects (as distinguished from those directed to officials), aside from obligations we voluntarily assume—by accepting positions of responsibility, owning property, becoming parties to contracts—we are under no special duties to make the legal system work. Being private persons, we are like army privates: our only duty is to obey.

Our choices as subjects are under our own control because they involve our own conduct (assuming that we can control our conduct); and in choosing we can be motivated by our own interests and values. And, when we choose to act or not act in disregard of a legal norm for reasons of expediency (say, because the costs of compliance exceed the costs of noncompliance) or conscience (say, because we think that the norm is wrong), we can do so more freely and openly than officials can do—or than our advisers can advise. This freedom results not only from the legal consideration that we are private citizens, unencumbered with official positions in the legal system, but also from the moral consideration that we are choosing on our own behalf and thus are risking only our own interests and values (which may, of course, include the interests and values of others). We may have to take the consequences (legal, social, economic, psychological) of our choices, but we are not obligated to justify them in terms of the interests and values of the legal system.

Our freedoms as subjects in making legal choices are considerable, but they are not unlimited. Precipitating events and applicable legal rules impose some constraints. Not all events permit factual choices: for example, we do not ordinarily choose to have accidents or to have someone hit us (although we may choose to act carelessly or provocatively). And norms that permit us to create legal relationships—like getting married, forming corporations, and making contracts—provide more freedom to choose whether we will apply them to ourselves (it is not illegal to remain single) than do norms that mandate how we are to behave—like those that tell us to pay our taxes, to perform our contracts, and to refrain from injuring other people (it is illegal to be a tax evader).

With permissive norms, we choose as subjects at two stages: whether to assume the constraints—marital, corporate, contractual—that the norm entails; and, if we freely choose to take on these constraints, whether we will actually use them to guide our conduct. (Will we observe our marital, corporate, or contractual vows?) In contrast, mandatory legal norms leave us no choice regarding their applicability to us, but only about whether we will actually apply them to our conduct. (Will we act with due care?) As to both kinds of norms, permissive and mandatory, if we choose not to be guided by them when they are applicable, we not only choose to be free riders who accept the benefits while rejecting the constraints of the legal system, but we also subject ourselves to the risk that some official, often at the prodding of another subject who feels injured by our free riding, will decide to apply those norms to us.

Officials

The decisions of officials are the teeth of the law. They bite in many ways, but always for the law.

Legal thinking, whatever its perspective, revolves around the making and justifying of official decisions as to whether legal norms will be applied to the conduct of subjects and other officials. These decisions and their justifications shape the ways in which subjects are subjected, officials officiate, advisers advise, and legislators make new law—and how legal scholars strive to explain all this. Understanding official decision making is essential to understanding legal thinking.

All of us, even officials, are subjects of the law in the same way, but the law's officials are officials in many different ways—as its interpreters, enforcers, administrators, and clerks—and make many different kinds of decisions. Compared with the legal choices of subjects, the legal decisions of officials are impersonal, accountable, and highly structured. And the stability and survival of a legal system calls for much more rigorous allegiances to the integrity of the system by its officials than by its subjects. A system can tolerate crooks on its streets, and even some in its corporate boardrooms, but not on its judicial benches.

Officials decide as agents of a legal system about the conduct of others. They are supposed to be guided by public interests and values, to be unaffected personally by their decisions, and to segregate their decisions from their private lives (requirements often hard to follow by part-time or unpaid officials). Legal norms tell officials how to proceed from event to decision, what they are empowered to decide, what they may take into account in deciding, and sometimes how they are expected to justify their decisions. The obligations of their positions require that they view the legal system internally to the system—seeing their decisions as parts of the system rather than as parts of their individual lives. By taking office they relinquish, as officials, freedoms that they take for granted as subjects: to choose not to be law abiding; to act despite a legal norm for their own reasons of expediency or conscience; to be accountable only to themselves.

Officials are the intermediaries between legislators and subjects. They take norms provided by legislators (say, about murder, negligence, contract) and match them against events generated by subjects (killings, accidents, business conversations). In preparation for this matching, officials conceptualize, or have conceptualized for them, legal situations from the ready-made norms and events presented to them. Then they do something that only officials can do. They make decisions, not choices, and they take official actions that determine—not whether the norms are logically applicable to the event, nor whether applying them will be fair or useful or probable (although the officials may use logic, fairness, or utility to arrive at and justify their decisions)—but whether the norms are applied to the events: whether, as a matter of law, killings are murders, accidents are results of negligence, or business conversations are contracts. And, according to some legal theory, officials, especially judges, are not supposed to have the option, available to subjects, of not applying a logically applicable legal norm. For officials, it is argued, the application decision is supposed to come automatically once the situation is properly conceptualized—a process that has been called mechanical or slot-machine jurisprudence.

Official discretion. To temper the rigor of their obligation to apply norms to events, judges and other officials may be allowed, or may take upon themselves, some freedom to make decisions regarding the meaning of the facts of events, and the influence of extralegal considerations. Officials are likely to ask themselves:

- How free am I to determine what this norm means? May I formulate my own meaning, or does the clarity of its language or definitive interpretation by a higher authority leave me no leeway?
- How free am I to determine what happened? May I formulate my own account of this event, or must I accept an account already made by other officials?
- How free am I to be influenced by the fairness or utility of applying this norm to this event? Are there authoritative instructions that limit my discretion?

The illustrations that follow, involving a police officer's official discretion about speeding and a prosecuting attorney's official discretion about homicide, provide some settings for these questions. (Official discretion is further discussed in Chapter 4, in which it figures as a form of legal freedom in tension with legal structures.)

The police officer (O) who gives me a ticket for exceeding the speed limit seems to have the straightforward task of connecting a clear-cut event, the fact that I drove at *x* miles per hour, with an equally clear-cut rule, the legal norm that it is unlawful to drive more than *y* miles per hour. If *x* is greater than *y*, the law has been violated. But we know that this sort of algebra gives a poor picture of O's real-life decision making.

The logical simplicity of O's job is complicated by background facts and by moral ideals and attitudes that are difficult for O to ignore. Most people share my behavior of driving faster than *y* on this highway, making it economically and politically expensive to prosecute all violators. The fairness of selecting some offenders (like me) for enforcement as examples (which is what O is probably doing) seems questionable; and, while published criteria for selection make a mockery of the legal rule, unpublished criteria will be suspect as discriminatory against disfavored groups (such as out-of-state, nonwhite, young, long-haired, or bearded drivers). Perhaps most inimical to the logical application of norm to event in this situation is the attitude of most people that it is all right to drive somewhat faster than *y* on this highway: they do not see such a violation as criminal.

It appears that O is in fact an official with substantial enforcement discretion. O's job is not simply to make mechanical (often electronic) connections between event and rule; rather, O is called upon to make subtle assessments about public interests and values—with economic, political, moral, and social implications—in deciding to whom the law is to be applied from among the many to whom it is logically applicable. And, of course, this discretion is shared with the many minor officials entrusted with the enforcement of the many other kinds of rules and regulations that defy being applied whenever their clear meanings say that they are applicable.

Now suppose that O is a prosecuting attorney assigned to a case like the one in Chapter 1 of householder A who, claiming that he mistook neighbor B for a burglar, shoots and kills B. Compared with my speeding violation (note that I am willing to cast myself as a speeder but not as a killer), this O will be working with events and norms that have less clear-cut meanings, but this O will also be working with background circumstances that interfere less with O applying an applicable norm to an event.

The most uncertain part of this event is A's state of mind when he shot B. Did A really think B was a burglar? Was this a reasonable assumption under the circumstances? Perhaps most crucially, did A really think he had a right to shoot burglars that he did not know to be armed? On the norm side, it is apparent that norms about when killings are excused as self-defense lack the numerical precision of speed limits and carry far more moral weight—unlike speeding, firing guns at people is not something that most people do or condone. While some might support A's claim of a right to protect one's home by shooting burglars, others might argue that it is of doubtful justice and utility to interpret the law so that resorts to deadly force are encouraged or condoned.

In deciding whether A should be prosecuted, O will be relatively free to make judgments about the facts of the event since the case is still in its initial stages. The courts of O's state will probably have interpreted the law of homicide to tell O whether the excuse of self-defense includes shooting someone one reasonably thinks is a burglar. And O's decision will be less influenced by what is common practice than was the police officer's decision in the speeding illustration. However, if A is a person of good reputation and if O believes that A is telling the truth as to why he shot B, O may exercise his or her discretion not to prosecute A, both because O may not view A as a criminal and because O may foresee difficulty in persuading a jury to convict A of a crime.

Justification of official decisions. While officials (being agents) are accountable for their legal decisions to their superiors in ways that subjects (being principals) are not accountable for their legal choices, the extent to which officials account to the public varies according to their offices. In general, enforcement, administrative, and ministerial officials are less publicly accountable than are the judges who interpret legal rules in order to apply them (and to inform other officials in applying them). An expectation that judges will publicly justify their decisions has been encouraged by the common law tradition that legal norms gradually take shape and work themselves pure in successive cases where judges compare and contrast the concept of the situation before them with concepts of earlier situations. In order for people to know what the law is, they need to have available not only the statutes that legislatures have enacted but also the decisions that judges have made and their justifications of what they have decided.

Justification of a legal decision calls for demonstration of why a particular legal norm should or should not be applied to a particular event. As has been suggested, in theory this is an exercise in connecting a legal meaning with an event. The norm provides the major premise and the event the minor premise of a syllogism: one who kills another with malice aforethought is guilty of murder. A killed B with (without) malice aforethought; therefore, A is (is not) guilty of murder. And this kind of justification becomes more nearly feasible after a succession of cases have earmarked some of the states of mind that do and do not constitute malice aforethought. But, as has also been suggested, judges may find it necessary to supplement legal meaning in justifying their decisions by appeals to what they perceive to be good social policy or fairness to the parties involved. (For example, it may have been decided that it is not good social policy to have the same standards for murder by police officers and by ordinary subjects; or that it is not fair to have the same standards of legal responsibility for those who are and are not mentally ill.) And of course, once previously extralegal factors of social policy or fairness are adopted as justifications for legal decisions, these factors may over time become part of the legal meaning of the norm and may cease to be extralegal in subsequent situations.

In summary, the obligations of officials to offer good reasons for their decisions encourage them to respect legal norms; at the same time, these obligations may also encourage officials to see themselves as free to interpret and to apply (or not apply) norms in light of what seems useful or fair. This paradox leads to the tensions in legal thinking that are the concern of the second part of this book. These tensions are between structures and freedom regarding what the law requires; between law and morals regarding what one ought to do; and between norms and facts regarding what one actually will do.

Part Two

TENSIONS IN LEGAL THINKING

Chapter Four

TENSION BETWEEN STRUCTURES AND FREEDOM REGARDING WHAT THE LAW REQUIRES

Earlier chapters suggested a tension between, on the one hand, the formal, structured parts of legal thinking—in which the norms and procedures of a legal system and one's positions within it seem to predetermine how one is to think—and, on the other hand, its informal, unstructured parts—in which individual freedom seems to be a law unto itself. Roles that cast judges as interpreters, not makers, of law do not seem to stop judges from making law; rules, such as speed limits, do not always rule subjects or officials; and logical connections between facts and legal norms often are overridden by appeals to fairness or social policy. In short, legal thinking seems to be a contradictory enterprise—at once both rule bound and unruly.

Tension between the formal structures of a system and the freedom of its individual subjects and officials—partially recognized in our own legal tradition by the division between law and equity—is not, of course, peculiar to Anglo-American legal thinking. Similar polarity between the claims of structures and freedom seems to pervade, and has given energy to, much of human culture. Witness, for example, the repeated use in ancient Egyptian art of separate symbols for stability and life (the former incorporating a balance, the latter a cross); the struggles in classical Greek drama between cosmic fate and human will; the divergent admonitions about obedience and choice in the Old and New Testaments; the competing Chinese concepts of "fa" (laws fixed beforehand) and "li" (doing justice); and, in art, architecture, music, and literature, the rival aesthetic attractions of attention to and emancipation from form—sometimes called the contest between harmony and invention. The dilemma is that structures can seem rigid and inhuman, as when a legal rule decrees that a starving person shall be punished for stealing food; but human freedom at its best is uncertain and at its worst can prove tragically capricious, as when it is exercised by a John Wilkes Booth or a Lee Harvey Oswald.

This chapter will look at the paradox of the law as structured freedom. First, legal thinking is disassembled into its structured and free parts. Then the parts are put together again to show how structures and freedom complement each other and how the concept of reasonability helps keep them in equilibrium. Since my concern here is not with particular problems, this chapter is less careful than was Chapter 3 to separate abstract and situational uncertainties.

Structures

In general, the structured parts of legal thinking are those traditionally taught in American law schools: positional structures of offices, roles, and functions; normative structures of legal rules, principles, and methods; and—the most difficult to teach—procedural structures that legal thinkers create out of language and logic, often with the help of precedents, to aid in identifying and interpreting legal rules and to conceptualize legal situations. In contrast, other parts of legal thinking less readily explained in terms of legal structures are largely left for on-the-job-learning—parts such as finding the objective facts of events from which to conceptualize legal situations; incorporating extralegal norms and subjective judgments into concepts of situations; and, as subjects, officials, or their advisers, actually making legal choices and decisions about situations. While law schools are tempering their preoccupation with structures by keying some learning not to abstract norms but to hypothetical events that require choices and decisions, and by exposing some students to clinical experiences with real people and real events, academic emphasis on structures will probably continue.

Understanding the positions from which and the norms and procedures with which legal thinking is done both provides the essential starting place for understanding legal thinking and can be effectively and economically imparted in the law school setting. However, the legal structures that this section examines are not confined to law school course offerings. Rather, they encompass whatever positions, norms, and procedures are embodied in a legal system to guide legal thinkers as they identify, interpret, and use legal norms in dealing with legal problems.

Positional structures: Offices, roles, functions

Chapter 1 focused on the several points of view—those of subject, official, adviser, legislator, legal scholar—from which legal thinking is done. Here, focus is on institutional positions rather than on people. Positions in a legal system here figure, not as individual points of view, but as constraints imposed on those who occupy the system's offices, assume its roles, or perform its functions.

The constraints of office restrict those who hold office, whether as officials or as legislators. In determining (whatever one's point of view may be) what ought to be considered a valid legal norm, what a norm ought to mean, and what ought (or is likely) to happen in a legal situation, one of the first questions to ask is: What are office holders called on to do by virtue of their offices? (For example, legislators are called upon to legislate but not, except as incidental to legislating, to interpret or apply the laws they make.) Offices define whether, when, where, and how their incumbents are empowered to make, find, construe, apply, and enforce legal rules; and they place on incumbents special abstract legal obligations that are coterminous with tenure in office and independent of particular events. Office holders undertake to discharge these obligations of office without fear or favor. Thus, offices—legislative, executive, and judicial—create structures that are more fixed beforehand than those created by other positions.

Roles differ from offices in being more widely distributed, less formally assumed, and more contingent on events. Subjects and advisers, as well as elected and appointed officials and legislators, have within the legal system institutional roles that restrict their freedom. Subjects not only have a general duty to obey the law but also may have special duties, such as paying taxes, serving on juries, and rendering military service. Lawyers are called officers of the court and undertake both to uphold the law and to represent their clients faithfully and zealously (undertakings that are not always compatible). People don and shed roles more readily than they do offices, and roles often depend on events: for example, while events, such as the absence or incapacity of a father or mother, may cause someone to assume the role of a child's parent, for one to assume the legal status of parenthood is a more formal matter.

Functions—things that a person functioning as a participant in a legal system is supposed to do—are even more informal, unstructured, and event bound (de facto) than are roles: for example, a servant may function as a parent without assuming the role of a parent. And the actual performance of the functions of offices and roles in a legal system is often delegated to subordinates, whose formal obligations are owed to their superiors rather than to the system. However, functions do limit the freedom of whoever happens to be performing them. The legislative function puts constraints on the investigative powers of legislative committees and their staffs by requiring them to relate what they do to the consideration of new legislation. The judicial function—constitutionally limited to "Cases" and "Controversies"—puts even narrower limits on what judges and their staffs are supposed to do. And despite the breadth of the executive function, it is not without boundaries: witness the Supreme Court decisions limiting the powers and privileges of the presidency.

Normative structures: Rules, principles, methods

In sorting out the materials of legal thinking, Chapter 2 referred to a legal system's rules, principles, and methods as legal norms to distinguish them from factual materials and from moral norms found in attitudes, obligations, and ideals. In this chapter, which concerns the tensions between freedom and legal structures, these legal norms are called normative structures, in order to distinguish them from positional and procedural structures and to bring out how they restrain freedom.

Compared with positional structures, a normative structure's content is more specific and more public and its authority is more general and more binding; compared with procedural structures, normative structures are more substantive. Legal rules, principles, and methods are supposed to be determined and promulgated before they are applied; in contrast, legal roles and functions, and sometimes even legal offices, may be shaped by incumbents as they go along—a theoretical difference that is reflected in the optimistic (and unrealistic) commonplace that ours is a government of laws, not men. And all who are within a legal system's jurisdiction are subject to its normative structures, whether or not they choose to be, whereas the constraints of a system's positional structures are felt mainly by its officials, who almost always may resign. Normative structures state directly how one should act (as do positional structures, although less directly); in contrast, procedural structures, the topic of the next subsection, state how one should proceed in understanding and employing normative structures—in short, how one should think before one acts.

A legal rule commanding us to do or not do something is what is likely to come to mind when we think (and complain) about how the law interferes with freedom, whereas legal principles and methods (if they are thought about at all) are seen as guiding conduct, but with a looser harness than do rules. Of course, to the extent that rules, principles, or methods state clearly, completely, and compellingly what is required, and to the extent that we are willing to accept and to act in accordance with what they say, it can be said that there is no tension: we simply allow the normative structures to dictate our choices and decisions. However, absent these ideal conditions, we find ourselves pulled between doing as we are told and doing as we see fit. A rule (say, a speed limit) may be clear and complete but may seem less than compelling because it generally is ignored by other subjects or officials. A principle (say, universal military service, or keeping religion out of public schools) may be clear, complete, and compelling but still unacceptable because it conflicts with a moral ideal (say, pacifism or evangelism) that the thinker puts above the law. And a method (say, applying to a case or issue the law of the state with the "most significant relationship" thereto) may fail to provide clear or complete guidance to a lawyer or judge.

When there are deficiencies in a legal norm's clarity, completeness, or authority, or in its moral or factual acceptability—which, unfortunately, happens quite often—subjects, officials, and advisers may be unable or unwilling simply to let the law be their guide; and then the question becomes: How free are they to do as they see fit? It does appear that they are not as free as they would be if the normative structure did not exist. Even a vague or incomplete structure provides some standards for making choices and decisions; and we disregard a legal norm, however disrespected or controversial, at the peril of being branded lawbreakers. For example, civic leaders have been disgraced when it was discovered that they had not bothered to pay all of their taxes.

Procedural structures: Language and logic

The points of view and normative materials detailed in Chapters 1 and 2 reveal substantive structures of positions and norms that, because their dictates can be neither blindly followed nor blithely ignored, are in tension with freedom. Similarly, the abstract and situational problems discussed in Chapter 3 bring to light procedural structures governing the uses of language and logic in resolving such problems. And these structures also are in tension with freedom because they limit but do not eliminate its exercise. These procedural constraints result from the need to use language in making statements about norms and facts, and the need to use both inductive and deductive reasoning in conceptualizing legal situations that combine general norms and particular events.

While constraints concerning the use of language are not peculiar to legal thinking, they call for special care in the legal context because legal systems, like religions and games, invest language with magical capabilities to create, populate, and govern the law's own universe. As we have seen, marriages, corporations, and other creatures of the law appear and disappear when language is used correctly: when the magic words are uttered by the right persons in the right settings. And some legal norms are codified in authoritative texts—constitutions, statutes, administrative rules, contracts—that are themselves magic words. These sacred texts can be construed by legal thinkers of all kinds and can be authoritatively interpreted by judges, but the words can be changed only by legislators. In contrast, uncodified legal norms—common law rules derived from customs and from precedents of prior judicial and administrative decisions—lack authoritatively legislated texts and thus permit more linguistic freedom than do codified norms. (To preserve this freedom in their constitutional law, the British have left their constitution unwritten.) However, unwritten law can take on quite rigid meaning, which may in practice restrict legal thinking more closely than does codified law: codes provide texts to which legal thinkers can return for fresh interpretations—which may be easier to obtain from judges than are changes in common law rules of long standing.

Norms always come to legal thinkers with some sort of legal meaning and may come with authoritative texts. Facts are different. While some facts are themselves verbal (for example, facts that the law classifies as slander, perjury, fraud, and contract), by themselves they have neither legal meaning nor authoritative text and thus do not generate linguistic constraints in the same way that norms do. But it is difficult to state the facts that are relevant to a legal problem without invoking a legal norm: How does one give a legal description of a highway collision except in light of norms about legal liability? Thus, linguistic constraints on our freedom to give the factual parts of legal problems legal meaning seem to become part of logical constraints on our freedom to produce concepts of legal situations by connecting facts with norms.

Legal situations need to be conceptualized in order to connect the specifics of events, past and present, with general structures. These connections are made both inductively, in deriving and refining general propositions about structures from past situations, and deductively, in determining the applicability of such general propositions to events in new situations. Thinkers are led to form hypotheses about the existence and meaning of legal structures and their applicability to events by examining how earlier situations have been resolved by judges and other legal thinkers—and by assuming that some general positional, normative, and procedural constraints were at work. These hypotheses about general constraints are then used to form the major premises of syllogisms that, by testing the fit of minor factual premises with major structural premises, draw conclusions about the facts of new cases. At both stages—inductive formulation of general propositions from the handling of past events and deductive use of generalities to categorize new events—a logic is at work that makes thinkers reject generalizations and particularizations that fail to make sense. They are suspicious of the creation of a hypothesis that seems ridiculously broad or narrow in light of prior cases, and they also question the application of an hypothesis that seems ridiculously expansive or constrictive in the light of a new case. Thus, they are constrained from doing as they please in connecting generals and particulars, not only by institutional positions, by the substantive content of legal norms, and by limitations on how language is used—but also by the need to avoid absurdity in the way these connections are made.

This felt need to avoid (in one's own and other's eyes) the appearance of absurdity in our concepts connecting general propositions and specific events is illustrated by a time-worn law school joke. A literal-minded common law judge had trouble deciding a case about the unauthorized taking by the defendant of the plaintiff's white horse because all the precedents that the judge could find involved horses of different colors. What makes this story useful in legal education is that to appreciate it one must recognize the absurdity of thinking that there are separate general rules about property rights in horses depending on their colors or—to put it another way—of thinking that it would be improper to conclude that there is a general rule against misappropriating another's horse, including a white horse, after a series of cases involving misappropriation of brown, black, and gray but no white horses. (And the story also shows that preoccupation with an irrelevant fact, like the horse's color, can divert a legal thinker's attention from the really interesting questions to ask about the taking of a horse: What sort of taking of a horse amounts to its misappropriation? How is borrowing a horse distinguished from stealing it? What was the defendant's state of mind when he or she took the horse? And how is that state of mind to be established?)

Freedom

Legal thinking entails coping with freedom as well as with structures. In the present context (of tension about what the law requires), freedom does not mean license to do as one pleases. Rather, legal freedom means that we may (and sometimes must) choose, decide, interpret, evaluate, or make other undetermined, largely subjective judgments in the course of dealing with legal problems. Opportunities for these exercises of legal freedom arise both because and in spite of legal structures. This section examines how the nature of freedom is affected by these structures, by the points of view of particular thinkers, and by the kinds of problems they consider. The following section examines in more detail how structures and freedom interact.

How structures affect freedom

In a sense, the free part of legal thinking is the part that, for some reason, structures do not control. It is when structures are clearly inapplicable, or can be interpreted away or simply ignored, that one seems to be free. But structures and freedom have a more complex relationship than that between doughnuts and their holes. As the preceding section made apparent, structures by themselves seldom solve legal problems. Neither one's position, nor legal norms that tell one what to do, nor the disciplines of language and logic can be depended on to remove all room for individual judgment. To delineate how structures affect the nature of freedom, I will examine here the several ways that judgment comes about: by unavoidably resorting to case-by-case handling of legal problems because of inherent limitations on what structures can do; by electing to introduce flexibility into structures to make them more "just"; and by "illegally" exercising freedom when structures are disregarded.

Structures leave wide areas of freedom because of what they do not purport to cover. Positional structures constrain directly and legally only those in positions: to the extent that we stay clear of positions, we stay clear of their constraints, although we may be sensitive to the constraints on the officials with whom we deal. Normative structures, while purporting to cast a wider net than do positional structures, often by their terms leave decisions about their meaning, applicability, and application to the discretion of officials. And, since the language and logic of legal thinking necessarily employ broad categories, they cannot automatically produce precise conclusions unaided by individual judgment; and they often seem more useful in justifying than in arriving at conclusions.

Akin to the freedom that results when structures do not purport to govern is the freedom that results from structural ambiguity. Concerning both kinds of freedom, thinkers are left no choice but to make judgments. Lacking unequivocal structural guidance, thinkers must themselves make specific what the structures require (e.g., how much care is "due care"? When does a contract become "unconscionable"?). This sort of unavoidable discretion so pervades legal thinking that we often fail to perceive it as freedom (we take it for granted as we do our freedom to make the decisions of everyday life—freedom that we appreciate only when it is lost because of ill health, economic exigency, imprisonment, or totalitarian government). And it is the freedom resulting from ambiguity that has led legal realists to argue that the "real" legal constraints on conduct are not legal structures but the factual consequences (going to jail or paying a fine or judgment) likely to follow from that conduct. They argue that structures are so ambiguous that they do in fact leave us free to do as we please, albeit at the risk of troublesome consequences—an argument that transforms much of legal thinking into economic thinking.

A somewhat different sort of freedom results when structures, instead of being too ambiguous to be meaningful, are too precise or clear-cut to make sense when literally applied to some events: say, a speed limit when an expectant mother is being rushed to a hospital. Another example, a favorite of legal philosophers, is whether a rule against men wearing hats in church applies to baby boys wearing bonnets. In order to rescue these structures from absurdity, freedom-creating qualifications are added. I referred earlier to how the Supreme Court qualified the Sherman Antitrust Act by interpreting it to mean that only unreasonable restraints of trade are unlawful, thereby shifting the focus in antitrust problems from legal structures to moral and economic evaluations, at least until precedents about what is and is not to be considered reasonable created new structures.

Coping in these ways with structures that seem too incomplete, loose, or tight involves tinkering with the structures in order to make them work better, but their authority remains unchallenged. In contrast, acting without regard to structures defies their authority, at least as to what is done. The tone of this defiance may cover a wide range: from quietly exceeding a speed limit (en route now to the movies rather than the hospital) along with almost everyone else on the road, to burning a draft card on the courthouse steps before television cameras. But in both cases the action is an assertion of freedom in spite of existing structures.

Factual freedom to disobey legal structures is included in this chapter both because structures are in fact often disregarded for many different reasons and in many different ways and in deference to Holmes and the legal realists, who tell us that as subjects we are always free to disregard structures and take the consequences. It should be noted, however, that while the law cannot eliminate the factual and moral freedom to disobey it, it also cannot recognize this freedom as a legal right. If enough people disobey enough legal structures, these structures will crumble.

When actual penalties for disobedience are likely to be minimal—when structures are difficult to enforce and command little respect, as was the experience with prohibition laws—there are strong disincentives to allowing structures to interfere with doing as one pleases. Then, about the only reward for obedience is one's self-image as a law-abiding person. And faithful compliance with some structures—such as tax laws—carries the danger that compliers will be taken advantage of by those who do not share their scruples. Thus, official disregard of structures is especially harmful to the rule of law, because it increases the danger that law-abiding citizens will be preyed on by those who disregard the law. And, as George Orwell warned us, perhaps the greatest harm is done by disregard—by legislators, teachers, and writers, as well as by officials—of the procedural structures of a legal system's language and logic; then, not only is our occasional conduct corrupted but also the very processes by which we think and communicate are put in jeopardy.

How points of view affect freedom

The free parts of legal thinking, in addition to being shaped by the structures with which they are in tension, are also shaped by the points of view of the thinkers and by the natures of their problems. One's options vary depending on where one sits and what one thinks about.

A legal system's subjects are, by definition, subject to its normative structures. But, as subjects, they occupy no official positions in the system and are not responsible for the purity of its language or logic: they remain free to be illiterate or illogical. And, as has been noted, the freedom of subjects includes the opportunity—in fact, the necessity—to choose whether legal norms or some other factors will determine their actions. Will signposts along the road or their own needs, conveniences, inclinations, or consciences determine how fast they drive? Of course, when subjects choose to follow the law—choose to be, for the moment at least, law-abiding persons—then, like other legal thinkers, they may still have some leeway in determining what the law requires: whether the speed limit does not apply to them because of some emergency, or even just because no one takes it seriously. But this intellectual freedom to decide what the law means (with the attendant risks of being wrong) is not the same as the more basic moral freedom to choose whether the law or something else will be one's guide. (For example, the intellectual freedom to determine whether the income tax law permits a particular deduction differs from the moral freedom to choose not to pay one's income tax—a difference recognized by the familiar distinction between tax avoidance, to accomplish which one hires a tax lawyer, and tax evasion, which may send one to prison.)

As subjects, people are free to make autonomous choices that express themselves and the kinds of persons they wish to be (e.g., choices concerning spouses and friends, jobs, clothes, and the use of spare time). But when they think legally, not as subjects but from other points of view that involve other people, they relinquish some of their autonomy, and their freedom takes on qualities that depend on their positions in and the workings of the legal system. Compared with the freedom of subjects to choose whether legal norms or something else will be their guides, other legal thinkers' freedom is less subjective, more easily avoided, and less exclusively in tension with normative structures. Rather than confronting purely personal choices, other legal thinkers make relatively objective—and, as has been noted, more clearly "legal"—decisions affecting other, often hypothetical, people. Whereas subjects are not free to sidestep their choices (since to live is to choose, although some would say it is also to react), those who occupy special positions can usually disengage themselves (judges call it "recusing" themselves) from having to make the decisions that go with their positions, if necessary by resigning. And, while as private persons people are free from most of the direct constraints of positions and procedures (but not of norms), when they take on public responsibilities—by becoming officials, advisers, legislators, legal scholars—they lose their purely private status and become more hedged in by the legal system, not only by its norms, but also by its offices, roles, and functions, and by its language and logic.

As noted in Chapter 1, officials of a legal system are not free to do other than to assume (like participants in a game) that events and the official responses they evoke have special legal meanings dictated by the system's structures. But, at the same time, officials are often allowed considerable freedom in arriving at and applying these legal meanings. As noted in Chapter 3, this freedom is called official discretion: the power, within limits, of judges, enforcement officials, administrators, and clerks to interpret, and to decide whether to apply, legal structures. This power may be granted expressly, or it may be the result of structural ambiguity. Sometimes official discretion is so open-ended that it appears capable of displacing structures. (Fear of unrestrained judicial discretion is reflected in the call for judges who are "strict constructionists," opposed to "judicial activism.") Nevertheless, official discretion is so much a part of legal systems that some legal theorists argue that it is really a kind of legal structure. Here, I will digress briefly to consider how free official discretion is.

The discretion allowed to officials, explicit or tacit, is less free than the freedom of subjects, as persons with free will to choose whether to obey the law, and is more akin to the freedom of subjects to interpret what the law means. When subjects decide not to be guided by the letter of the law, not out of defiance of the law but simply as a matter of what they consider its sensible interpretation, they are, in effect, doing their own officiating. This difference between choice and discretion explains why, to a twentieth-century American, it sounds odd to say that one has discretion to decide whom one marries; while marrying is a legal act, it is also, more fundamentally (as our law recognizes), an exercise of the freedom of an autonomous person. In contrast, the idea of discretion includes notions of prudence and good judgment—being discreet—with the possibility of review by some higher authority and the employment of standards to avoid abuses of discretion. But, even though official discretion is less free than personal choice, for present purposes it seems to belong on the side of freedom rather than structures, because it is a human being, albeit an official, who decides—not an office, or a rule, or a logic. And predicting how officials will in fact exercise their freedom to decide is, as Holmes insisted, the preoccupation of much legal thinking from most perspectives, with the possible exception of the legislative perspective.

Legislators are free in a unique way because they can create new normative structures. Because they are not supposed to legislate regarding events that have already happened (although they may investigate such events as part of their legislative function), and because they can change the legal powers of officials regarding future events, they are less concerned than other legal thinkers with predicting how official discretion will be exercised. However, legislators are constrained as to the new structures that they can create both by the constitutional, statutory, and other limits of their legal powers and by the practical need when legislating to employ language and logic more or less correctly.

Advisers are the least free of all legal thinkers. They are governed by all of the kinds of structures described in this chapter. They lack the autonomy of subjects, the discretion of officials, the creative powers of legislators, and the objective stance of legal scholars. Among the cast of legal thinkers, they are the most preoccupied with predicting official action. Freedom for advisers must be found in how they use their opportunities to influence the choices and decisions of the subjects and officials they advise. Theirs is a professional freedom to utilize structures and official discretion in order to accomplish their clients' objectives. That this is a significant, although narrow, freedom is demonstrated by the difference between the consequences of good and bad legal advice, and by the extent to which subjects and officials rely on (and pay for) professional advice in making their choices and decisions.

Legal scholars, being as such positioned on the sidelines of a legal system, are free of direct constraint from its positional and normative structures but are closely bound by its structures of language and logic—since these are their stock in trade. Their freedom does not concern whether and how to obey and enforce the law, or whether to create new law, or how to protect and further the interests of clients. Rather, their freedom, academic and literary, is to choose how most accurately and clearly to pass on to others, in classrooms and in what they write, an understanding of how a legal system works and how it might be improved. As with advisers, their freedom is professional, and the way this freedom is exercised is part of what makes effective or ineffective teaching and writing.

How problems affect freedom

Chapter 3 divided legal problems—the uncertainties about which legal thinkers think—into two large categories, abstract and situational. Abstract legal problems are concerned with identifying and giving meaning to legal structures, most typically legal norms, before they have become involved with actual events. In contrast, situational legal problems assume that the legal structures have been identified and interpreted in the abstract, and that any uncertainties concern the applicability of such structures to actual events and whether the structures will actually be applied to these events. Problems of applicability of structures to events require thinkers to conceptualize legal situations, which combine structures, events, and other normative and factual materials. Problems of actual application require subjects and officials to make choices and decisions about how they will act.

Here the focus is on how this division between abstract and situational problems affects the nature of a legal thinker's freedom. Freedom seems to be shaped by differences between both the starting and ending places of the two kinds of problems: by differences between the kinds of initial assumptions thinkers can or must make about structures and events, and by differences between the kinds of conclusions their thinking is directed toward.

In separating law from not-law and in searching, within and without the law, for abstract meanings of legal structures, thinkers assume that the structures are those of a functioning legal system with some valid, meaningful structures. Thus, abstract thinkers are both free and not free: they are free to discover which structures are valid and to give these structures meanings; but, valid structures having been identified and interpreted, they are not free to reject or ignore their validity or meaning. In contrast, situational thinkers at the outset (when they set out to connect events with structures in order to develop concepts of legal situations) start with assumptions about the abstract validity and meaning of structures. However, in the process of matching events with structures, situational thinkers have considerable freedom in particularizing the given abstract meanings. And, as we have seen, at the final stage of situational thinking—when the issue is whether structures will actually be applied to events—subjects are free to choose whether they will obey the law, and officials often have discretion to decide whether they will enforce it. As problems move from abstract to situational, thinkers become freer to loosen the bonds of structures. Abstract legal thinking becomes nonsensical, as readers of Lewis Carroll's *Alice in Wonderland* find, unless structures are taken seriously. But in situations the danger of nonsense arises less from playing fast and loose with structures, in the manner of a Red Queen, than from being blind to real-life consequences of applying structures to events—like applying hats-off rules to baby boys in bonnets.

Abstract and situational problems share a need to deal with structures, although in different ways, but by definition only situational problems are tied to actual events. Thus, when legal problems are abstract, as they are for legislators and legal scholars (and for subjects and officials and their advisers when they prepare for future situational problems), thinkers are free to create their own hypothetical events to test how their abstractions will work. But when actual events make a problem situational, freedom changes. In conceptualizing legal situations, thinkers are free to interpret events in the light of structures (and structures in the light of events), but they are not free to deal with actual events in the way law teachers deal with hypotheticals. Tampering with the evidence is a serious offense. Situational problems start from events in the real world—the transactions and collisions of everyday life that are beyond the freedom of subjects or officials or their advisers to change—although, by the astute selection and use of evidence, subjects, officials, and advisers can, of course, change how events and their circumstances are perceived.

The quality of legal freedom varies with the kinds of conclusions that thinkers are seeking to reach. Abstract speculation at the constitutional levels (speculation aimed at separating law from not-law) is unconstrained either by actual events or by most legal structures other than those of language and logic. Abstract interpretation of legal norms below the constitutional level, when the thinker is seeking legal meaning rather than legal status, is similarly unrestrained by events; and, when done by thinkers other than officials, it is also unrestrained by positional structures. But all abstract interpretation is closely bound by normative and procedural structures. In construing statutes law teachers can create facts and assume roles as they please, but they must treat the words of the statute with respect and be careful about how they use language and logic.

When the objective of the thinker is to conceptualize legal situations by connecting actual, newly happened events with norms already established as legal and already clothed with abstract meanings, the thinker's freedom shifts. Now its province becomes the selection of "controlling" precedents and of "relevant" evidence about details of the new events and their circumstances that will make the evidence seem to fit (or not fit) the norms, and these norms are now reinterpreted in contexts provided by the precedents and the evidence about the new events. It is at this stage, when major premises in the form of general legal norms and minor premises in the form of accounts of specific events are stated and fitted together, that lawyers and judges do most of their legal thinking.

Finally, at the bottom line, when subjects and officials opt whether to apply the norms to the events, freedom takes on a still different quality. It becomes a matter of subjects making choices for themselves about whether they will be guided by the law, and of officials, acting on behalf of the legal system, exercising legal discretion about whether they will enforce the law. And, while the vicarious decisions that officials make doing their jobs are more consequential in terms of the law's efficacy, the autonomous choices that subjects make living their lives are more truly free. As human mortality seems to be an absolute in the realm of nature, so human freedom to disobey human law—and to suffer the consequences of disobedience—seems to be an absolute in the realm of society.

Structured Freedom

The preceding sections have kept the structured and the free parts of legal thinking separate except to consider how legal structures, along with legal perspectives and problems, help shape legal freedom. But this separation is artificial. Most legal thinking, like most other kinds of thinking, oscillates between being guided by structures and exercising freedom—between following trails and bushwhacking on one's own. While legal thinkers find guidance in positions and norms and in language and logic, at the same time they choose, decide, interpret, evaluate, predict, and make other individual judgments. This section will put structures and freedom back together again in order to see how they complement one another, and how they are brought together by reason.

Structures and freedom as parts of one whole

A system is not a legal system unless the absolute freedom of its subjects and officials is somehow limited by its legal structures. But a legal system will be too rigid to work at all, or to work justly or humanely, unless its participants are free to adapt existing structures and to create new structures. And, according to American constitutional doctrine, a system will also fail to be truly legal unless the freedom of legislators and officials to create and adapt subordinate structures is limited by higher constitutional structures.

Structures and freedom complement each other in different ways at three levels of the hierarchy that makes up a constitutional legal system. At the working level of ordinary events and transactions that do not get into the courts, subjects and minor officials, sometimes with the aid of advisers, choose and decide within limits set by structures that they call the law. At the middle or governmental level of cases and legislative sessions, higher officials (judges and administrators) and legislators exercise their freedom to adapt and to change these structures, to create new law. And at the constitutional level, judges review both working-level structures and officiating (e.g., the conduct of police during an arrest) and middle-level exercises of adaptive and legislative freedom in the light of a higher law. Although this higher law is embodied in a constitution, judges are free to adapt it to new situations, thereby creating new constitutional law (but still under the old constitution), which may expand or contract governmental power. (However, not all constitutional legal systems provide for judicial review of the constitutionality of legislation.)

At the working level of a legal system, both subjects and officials move between being guided by structures and exercising freedom, but in different ways. As a subject, one sees structures as outcroppings on a field of otherwise pervasive, undifferentiated freedom, and one tends to think along the following lines:

- I am free to do as I please, absent constraining structures, and structures are mainly useful to keep others from interfering with my freedom.
- I am free to interpret structures to determine whether they are applicable in situations to which I am a party, although I may resort to help from an adviser.
- And, even though structures are applicable in these situations, I am free to choose whether these structures or something else will determine my conduct—a choice usually made more on the basis of my factual predictions about how officials will exercise their freedom than on legal interpretations of structures.

In contrast, officials, particularly minor ones, tend to see a field of structures with isolated outcroppings of freedom. In interpreting structures they look not for ways to avoid structural coverage of the situations before them as subjects typically do but for the extent of their own authority to act in the situations and for the extent of their own discretion to decide whether and how to act. This discretion is the chief freedom of minor officials, often freeing them to apply structures selectively to subjects (for example, to select which speeders will be ticketed). Unlike subjects, officials are not free to disregard structures in favor of their own interests or values; nor, of course, are they free to act on predictions about their own exercises of freedom, although they may attempt to predict how higher officials will exercise their freedom.

Above the working level, subjects and officials rely more heavily on advisers, and legal education concentrates on preparing lawyers to think in terms of cases. The middle or governmental level is characterized by the clear-cut freedom of legislators to create new structures, limited only by their statutory and constitutional powers, and by the less clear-cut freedom of judges and senior administrators to adapt existing structures to new situations. At the middle level, situations are more fully conceptualized than at the working level, and thinkers approach structures and freedom in a more balanced, professional way: thinking is less dominated by self-centered assumptions of subjects about their freedom or by job-oriented preoccupations of minor officials with the structures they administer. While the freedom of officials to make discretionary decisions and of subjects and their lawyers to predict these decisions remain important, the more structured—that is, more "legal"—freedom to interpret the law and to adapt it in new situations takes center stage at the middle level. Adaptation of structures to events is usually accompanied with some adaptation of events to structures: there is a tailoring of facts to fit the law as well as of law to fit the facts.

This two-way adaptation process is more respectful of structures than are exercises of official discretion because it is less arbitrary and depends less on individual judgment. It does not, of course, obviate the need for judgment, but it replaces a judgment call of pure decision ("You're out!") with a more abstract judgment of interpretation ("The rule about when a player is 'out' in a situation like the one before us means . . ."), although it is usually an interpretation that leads ineluctably to a decision one way or the other (that the player is either out or not out). Legal realists argue that decisions purporting to be the products of dispassionate interpretation are usually exercises of more or less arbitrary discretion, with structural interpretation appended by way of justification. Even if this argument is accepted, it is still significant that judges feel constrained to accord structures the respect of at least appearing to make them the "deciding factor." And even after-the-fact justifications help subsequent judges and lawyers to interpret structures and to connect them with events in new situations and may reduce the freedom of judges to decide later cases according to their own discretion.

At the constitutional level, judges review the legitimacy of lower-level structures and official acts: the legal powers of officials to apply structures and exercise discretion, of judges and administrators to interpret, adapt, and apply structures, and of legislators to create structures in the first place. Structural tests for legitimacy are based on the words of the legal system's constitution and on prior judicial interpretations of these words. The constitution's text can be changed only by amendment, but, as has been noted, the constitution's words can be and are judicially reinterpreted. These constitutional structures, which restrain officials, not subjects, are supposed to mark the outside legal limits of governmental power for a particular legal system. They usually come into play in situations only after questions of structural interpretation and applicability have been resolved, because it is customary for a court to consider the constitutionality of a structure only after it has concluded that the structure is, apart from the constitution, legally applicable in the situation before the court. Thus, in a constitutional case there may be a dual interpretive freedom: to interpret the challenged structure or its applicability; and then, if necessary, to interpret the constitution. If the challenged structure was not legally applicable in the situation, constitutional interpretation is not needed.

Structures and freedom brought together by reason

In adapting and creating legal structures within constitutional limits—in exercising the necessary, structured freedom essential for the functioning of a legal system, as distinguished from the optional, unstructured freedom to choose to disregard structures—legal thinkers need ways of knowing how much freedom they are legally permitted. The usual formula to describe permissible exercises of freedom is to say that they must be reasonable or due. Our law has many rules of reason that transfer effective guidance from structures fixed beforehand to what is judged reasonable under the circumstances, although such judgments may not be wholly unstructured when conduct and its consequences are judged according to some standard of rationality. Examples of legal rules of reason include the negligence rule against acting without due care, the antitrust rule forbidding unreasonable restraints of trade, and the constitutional rule outlawing state action against subjects without due process of law.

Beneath the textual simplicity of rules of reason lie formidable complexities and ambiguities. Who is to judge what is reasonable and at what stages of legal problems? Which circumstances will be counted and which standards applied? And, most fundamentally, in what sense is reasonability to be assessed: is the concern with the reasonability of conduct, meaning, or results?

While legal thinkers of all sorts make judgments about reasonability in all three of these senses, they do so with data, purposes, and attitudes about structures that vary with the thinkers' perspectives and the stages at which they enter problems. For example, initial judgments are made by subjects (sometimes with the help of advisers) about whether ordinary conduct (like driving an automobile) shows lack of due care and about whether business conduct (like making a long-term contract with a customer) amounts to an unreasonable restraint of trade; but these judgments may later be reviewed by judges, juries, and other officials. Similarly, initial decisions about the "dueness" of legal processes used against subjects are made by officials—often quite minor ones, like police officers—but these decisions may eventually be reviewed by the Supreme Court. While the formal legal question about reasonability in each of these contexts remains the same from event to final decision, what is actually thought about goes through several changes. Appraisals of the reasonability of driving practices, business contracts, and police methods, respectively, are made differently by drivers and juries, by business persons and antitrust enforcers, and by police officers and judges. But even more significant than the points of view of the appraisers are the kinds of reasonability that are being appraised.

Reasonability of conduct

In determining what happened and in judging how what happened connects with standards of reasonability, legal thinkers use reasonability to mediate between structures and freedom. For example, in a negligence case a jury is asked to decide whether an actor acted as a reasonably prudent person would have acted under the circumstances. To make this decision, jury members hearing a case involving an automobile accident are supposed first to make factual findings about what the actor actually did (how fast was he driving, had he been drinking, who hit whom) and under what circumstances (regarding the condition of his car, the road, the weather), and then to make a judgment about whether the actor's conduct under these circumstances fits the jury members' ideas of what a reasonable person would have done. In short, jury members are supposed to form and match pictures in their minds of what the actor did and what he should have done. They create their own structures, their individual mental pictures of reasonable prudence in this situation, to guide their freedom to decide. In this process of matching perceptions of conduct and ideas about what is reasonable, the following kinds of difficulties can arise:

- How far afield should one go in considering surrounding circumstances: in the automobile accident case is it relevant that the actor had just quarreled with his wife?
- To what extent should one take into account the actor's individual characteristics: if the actor is nearsighted, should the standard be that of a myopic but reasonably prudent person?
- Should the jury's conclusions about reasonability be reviewable by someone else? Should a judge be empowered to reject as unreasonable a jury's verdict about what is reasonable?

Reasonability of meaning

In dealing with the reasonability of conduct, the applicability of a structure to the conduct is assumed, and the end product is a decision about that conduct. In dealing with the reasonability of meaning, it is the conduct that is assumed, and the end product is a judgment about whether it is reasonable to apply legal structures to this conduct. This difference is illustrated by comparing the reasonability at issue in the negligence case above, which asks whether a driver has used due care (i.e., driven as a reasonably prudent driver would have driven), with the reasonability at issue in an antitrust case, which asks whether a contract is an unreasonable restraint of trade. In the antitrust case, the inquiry is not whether the defendant in making the contract acted as a reasonably prudent businessperson would act, but whether the contract, which here can be called the event, unreasonably restrains trade: whether the Sherman Act logically applies to this event and gives it special legal meaning. Instead of focusing on how the event happened and whether the defendant acted reasonably, as evidence in the negligence case does, evidence in the antitrust case will be mainly about the consequences of the event and whether it is reasonable for the law to permit them.

Reasonability of meaning is used to test the interpretations, abstract or situational, of legal structures, the connections of structures with events, and the conceptualizations of total legal situations—structures, events, and circumstances—that give legal meaning to events. Reasonability of meaning is what is usually the goal of legal reasoning, and it is obviously more legalistic and less responsive to what actually happens in the real world—less "sensible"—than is reasonability of conduct.

Reasonability of results

When neither the reasonability of conduct nor the reasonability of meaning is in question, a third kind of reasonability can still come into play to determine whether it makes practical sense to apply structures to events. At this stage, when facts about an event and its circumstance have been determined and a structure has been interpreted and found applicable, there remains a final freedom to choose or decide whether it is reasonable for the structure to govern what a subject or official does. (For more on this topic, see Chapter 6.)

We have seen that at the level at which subjects choose whether to obey an applicable law and minor officials decide whether to enforce it, practical reasonability is assessed in terms of what action by officials and their superiors can reasonably be predicted. It does not seem to make much sense to obey or enforce a law that higher officials do not seem to take seriously. But if higher officials are presented with cases involving clearly applicable structures, it is more difficult for these officials to avoid applying the structures than it is for subjects, who can ignore them, or for minor officials, who can look the other way. At these higher levels, if reasonability of results is invoked to ease the rigors of the letter of the law, it is not on the basis of predictions about whether the law will be enforced but by appeals to some broad grounds of the public good. For example, for the rule that plaintiffs who are themselves negligent cannot recover from negligent defendants (the contributory negligence rule), courts in several states have substituted a more flexible and "fair"—and therefore more uncertain and difficult to apply—rule that apportions the cost of accidents among the parties on the basis of their comparative negligence. Similarly, constitutional guarantees of due process and equal protection of the law are sometimes used by judges to avoid socially or politically undesirable consequences of applying applicable legal structures. For example, judges have used the due process clause both to invalidate social legislation that seemed to interfere unreasonably with business freedom and to outlaw police practices that seemed to interfere unreasonably with personal freedom.

Reasonability in its several senses—of conduct, legal meaning, and results—seems to be an idea that both structures and frees legal thinking. It structures appraisal of conduct by providing a standard against which to measure conduct and its appraisal but leaves the appraiser free to create his or her own standard. It sets knowable, communicable limits to legal meaning but also interjects flexibility and good sense into the process of legal reasoning. And, without abdicating enforcement of the law to the interest or caprice of the enforcer, it saves the law from mechanical, inhuman applications of structures to events. In short, the tension created by the seeming polarity of structures and freedom is kept in equilibrium, and even made useful and energizing, by the multifarious idea of reasonability.

To close this chapter on structures and freedom, consider the following scenario: I want to walk from A to B, a trek I have not made before, by the fastest, easiest route. At A a local resident directs me to a well-trodden footpath marked, "To B, 12 miles." It would be reasonable for me to relinquish my freedom to the extent of following the path. But if the path forks or disappears, or leads into a thicket or over a cliff, it becomes reasonable for me to reassert my freedom. And I will probably use my freedom in a search for something else (another person, another path, a water course) to guide me—although if I am confident of my sense of direction, I may seek my own way. Eventually, I will probably get to B having made an uncountable number of oscillations—mediated, it is to be hoped, by reason—between relying on structures and on freedom, between being guided and finding my own way. Thinking about what the law requires is often such a journey.

Chapter Five

TENSION BETWEEN LAW AND MORALS

Tension between structures and freedom about what the law requires would exist even if the law were a closed system isolated from outside influences. But, of course, legal systems (unlike games and some religions) are not closed; and external forces, both normative and factual, are at work creating their own tensions with the law. To the extent that these external forces are normative, the terms *morals* and *moral norms* are here used to designate them. Chapter 2, in describing the materials for legal thinking, listed several sources of moral norms: attitudes actually prevailing in particular communities (mores); obligations assumed by those in positions of trust (ethics); obligations assumed by individuals for their own reasons, religious or otherwise (conscience); and ideals of right and wrong for governments in governing and subjects in dealing with each other (justice and fairness).

Tension between legal norms and norms generated by moral attitudes, obligations, and ideals—and not yet given the status of legal norms—can be characterized as tension between following legal procedures and paying attention to moral substance. Stated another way, it is tension between the substantive arbitrariness of law, which assumes that by legal fiat shades of gray can be divided into black and white, and the procedural arbitrariness of morality, which assumes that usable norms can be directly derived from such elusive standards as public attitudes, the ethics and consciences of individuals, or the ideals of justice and fairness. Legal norms are by definition parts of a specific legal system. The system provides procedures to identify and interpret its norms and to determine their legal applicability and how they will actually be applied to events, and it provides a corps of officials to administer these procedures and a cadre of professional advisers to aid subjects and officials, all to the end of clarifying what the law requires. In contrast, moral norms, lacking both procedural context and administrative apparatus, are almost all substance: they declare what ought to be done, but provide no official procedures or personnel for enunciating, changing, adjudicating, or enforcing their commands, or for dispelling vagueness or inconsistency in what they require.

It is true that moral norms can be said to have a procedural aspect, which itself may be moral or immoral, with regard to the integrity of the ways they were generated: Were prevailing community attitudes formed naturally, or by propaganda and manipulation? Did individuals undertake their obligations of ethics and conscience freely and wholeheartedly or under duress and subject to reservations? Were the ideals of justice and fairness evolved to secure the good life for all, or (as some Marxists claim) to obscure and perpetuate class differences—or to promote the values of a particular, predominantly Western or European culture? Thus, while the term *validity* is ordinarily reserved for legal norms, there is a sense in which moral norms can also be valid or invalid. However, when this chapter refers to procedure and validity, it will ordinarily mean legal rather than moral procedure and validity.

The problems of the vagueness and inconsistency of moral norms, and of who is to select, interpret, and apply them in legal situations, have led some legal theorists to argue that the law should be kept free of morals. But in a working legal system, as distinguished from a theoretical one, a sharp separation between law and morals is seldom practicable. Moral attitudes, obligations, and ideals are often ambivalent and ambiguous and resort to them by judges and other officials creates the danger that individual moral idiosyncrasies will be imposed on the law. Nevertheless, they often seem to tell us—more concretely, persuasively, and humanely than do legal norms by themselves—what the law ought to be and to mean, and how it ought to connect with events and to guide conduct.

In addition to detailing the different kinds of morals, Chapter 2 also described the factual judgments made by legal thinkers about what is prudent in light of the probable consequences to relevant interests and values. And Chapter 3 divided legal problems into four stages: (1) the validation stage of identifying a norm as a legal norm; (2) the interpretation stage of giving a legal norm abstract meaning in light of its text, purpose, and history; (3) the situational stage of connecting a legal norm with an event and determining whether the norm ought to be applied (is applicable) to the event; and, finally, (4) the choice or decision stage of determining whether normative authority or factual prudence will govern the event.

This chapter deals with tension experienced in the first three of the stages—tension between law and morals over whether legal or moral standards will be used in determining a legal norm's validity, meaning, and applicability. The following (and concluding) chapter deals with tension experienced in the final stage, tension between norms and facts over whether respect for normative authority or a factual judgment about what is prudent will prevail in choosing and deciding whether a norm will actually be applied to an event. (Of course, if a thinker skips the first three stages and thinks only about actual application of a legal norm to event, tensions between law and morals as well as between norms and facts may affect that choice or decision.)

Tension Concerning Legal Validity

Morals can come into tension with law concerning the legal validity of norms by working either to negate or to affirm that validity. Legal norms, apparently valid because they were generated in accordance with legal procedures, may have their legal status negated if their substantive provisions or the procedures by which they were produced conflict seriously with community mores, obligations of ethics or conscience, or ideals of justice or fairness. Conversely, norms with dubious legal pedigrees may have their legal status affirmed if they are in substantive accord with important moral attitudes, obligations, or ideals. Thus, moral negations of legal validity may be either procedural (say, failure to provide a fair hearing) or substantive (say, state discrimination on the basis of race); but moral affirmations of validity are confined to substance. In other words, providing a fair procedure does not validate an otherwise invalid proceeding. And validity is more easily negated on moral grounds than it is affirmed on those grounds. It is easier to argue that a norm with a legal pedigree is so morally wrong that it is not law at all than it is to argue that a norm without legal pedigree must be law because it is so morally right.

Invalidation of legal norms on moral grounds

Legal invalidity on moral grounds of an otherwise correct and applicable norm of the legal system of State A can be asserted by subjects of A seeking to avoid application of the norm to them; it can also be asserted by officials of State B seeking to avoid applying the A norm in a B proceeding. (Recall that Chapter 2 discussed the possibility that one state may, and may be required to, respect a legal norm of another state.) Subjects usually claim that the norm violates their constitutional rights, whereas officials of State B usually appeal to a strong public policy of B. Either sort of attack may be on procedural or substantive grounds. This subsection first examines how subjects make moral attacks on the norms of their own legal systems and then how officials make these attacks on the norms of other systems.

Constitutional and other attacks by subjects

In the Anglo-American legal tradition, attacks by subjects on the morality of the procedures by which norms sought to be applied to them were generated are usually cast in terms of due process. This broad concept has evolved in large part from middle-class opposition in the seventeenth and eighteenth centuries to absolute government and from the political theories, like those of Locke and Jefferson, that were formulated to justify this opposition. Using this concept, subjects may claim that, regardless of a legal norm's content, the way in which it was created—a statute enacted, a regulation adopted, judicial jurisdiction asserted, evidence gathered, or a trial conducted—was so contrary to the mores of the community, to the ethical obligations of lawyers and officials, or to the ideals of justice and fairness, as to invalidate the norm that resulted.

The right to due process is a protection for subjects against morally offensive acts done on behalf of governments, not against private acts of other subjects done on their own behalf (although what starts as private action may escalate into state action if officials are persuaded to act officially or if subjects act under color of law or of sanctioned custom). In recent years, the right to due process most frequently has been asserted by those accused of crimes. Community attitudes sometimes turn against this right when it seems to be a way for alleged criminals to escape punishment, although most of us want due process when we are accused of crimes. An extreme example of lack of due process, which almost everyone would acknowledge should invalidate a conviction, is when the accused has been tortured to force a confession; at the other end of the spectrum are cases in which "the constable blundered" by failing to observe the legal niceties in gathering evidence.

To the extent that the specifics of procedural due process are set forth in a system's constitution, statutes, or judge-made rules—as is the case, for example, with rights to trial by jury, assistance of counsel, and opportunity for cross-examination—these specifics assume legal (as distinguished from purely moral) status, and it can be said that subjects do not go outside the law in their appeals. But sometimes subjects make and judges accept arguments that the right to due process is not confined to rights already incorporated into the law and that it encompasses protection against any way of proceeding that "shocks the conscience" (Justice Frankfurter's broad statement of due process, which shocked the legal sensibilities of Justice Black in the 1952 case, *Rochin* v. *California*, involving evidence obtained by a stomach pump). And, even when due process is legally defined, moral considerations may influence its applicability in borderline situations—such as whether those accused of minor offenses have a right to counsel.

Substantive (as distinguished from procedural) attacks by subjects on the morality of legal norms carry the law-morals confrontation outside the workings of a legal system into a broader arena, where the issue is whether moral boundaries are to be set upon what the law can do: Are some laws so substantively immoral that, notwithstanding proper legal pedigrees, they are not law at all? Lawyers and judges often are qualified to spot procedures within their own legal system that are too out of line with morality to be called legal, but they are less qualified to identify the kinds of human behavior that are so immoral that any law mandating or permitting this behavior should be invalidated.

For example, the half-century between the 1880s and the 1930s saw many judicial decisions invalidating social legislation, such as laws against child labor, too low wages, and excessive working hours—legislation that employers and judges considered deprivations of liberty and property without due process of law. But since the 1930s judges have been reluctant to use the due process clause to justify substituting their own moral judgments for those of state and federal legislatures, although this reluctance is less marked when personal, rather than business, rights are at stake. As we have seen, judges are still making moral judgments that invalidate procedurally legal norms under the equal protection clause and the bill of rights, but these parts of the U.S. Constitution authorize the courts to make more restricted moral attacks on legislation—here also with greater concentration on personal than on business rights—than the due process clause was held to authorize in the older cases. While the contours of equal protection remain uncertain, it seems to be a concept of sufficient objectivity to save the courts from having to rely as exclusively as they do under substantive due process on their own moral judgments.

It is difficult, however, for judges to avoid the role of moral censors when the law employs moral norms to define what is legal. And it is not only constitutional and criminal law questions that cast judges in this role. In the arena of private law, in which legal norms are created by private transactions to which both subjects and governments may be parties, validity of these private norms can often be attacked on moral grounds. For example, under the Uniform Commercial Code, judges may refuse to enforce contracts they find to be unconscionable. And many kinds of business transactions—including those reorganizing and combining corporations, trading in securities, and using another's business reputation—can be invalidated if they are found to violate the moral (and, in these cases, legal) ideal of fairness.

Attacks by officials of other states

Because legal situations often have connections with more than one state (the term *state* here includes not only a state of the United States but also any other sovereign state), a branch of law called conflict of laws has developed to determine when states will assume jurisdiction (power) to adjudicate multistate situations, which states' rules of decision will be chosen to govern these situations, and when out-of-state adjudications will be recognized as legally valid. Thus, in addition to the internal rules that legal systems apply in purely local situations with no out-of-state elements, legal systems also have special rules about jurisdiction to adjudicate, choice of law, and recognition of foreign judgments. A state of the United States is constitutionally limited by the due process clause to asserting jurisdiction over situations with which it has "minimum contacts" (according to the 1945 decision in *International Shoe Co.* v. *Washington*) and is constitutionally required by the full faith and credit clause (Article IV, Section 1) to recognize judgments of other U.S. states unless to do so would interfere with its important interests.

When an attempt is made in State B to apply a legal norm or enforce a judgment of State A, officials of B are likely to balk if they think that the result is likely to offend mores, obligations, or ideals that are highly regarded in B. Serious moral differences, procedural or substantive, between the legal norms of A and B are usually the result of differences in their cultural or industrial development, political or economic theories, or religious beliefs. But even states without these large-scale differences may find moral reasons for declining to recognize each other's legal norms or judgments. For example, differences in family law—such as differences in rules involving marriage status and marital property, or the custody, support, legitimation, and adoption of children—often result in officials in B declining to accept what A has declared to be the law, even when A and B are both states of the United States. Moral attitudes may also vary from state to state about such issues as usury, gambling, alcohol and drug control, Sunday business, birth control, abortion, gun control, school prayers, environmental protection, and racial integration.

Consider the following hypothetical pair of states with laws that reflect different attitudes about the ease with which marriages can be legally dissolved. The law of A provides that its courts will grant divorces on the petition of a resident of A without requiring the appearance of or the giving of notice to the other party, and without requiring the proof of any grounds for the divorce. The law of B provides that its courts will grant divorces on the petition of a resident who has made a good-faith effort to notify the other party and who satisfies the court of the existence of at least one of several stated grounds for divorce. Suppose that H and W marry in State B and live there together for several years. Then they separate and H moves to A, where he secures a divorce without any effort to notify W and without proof of any grounds. H dies, leaving property in B. W asks a B court to declare that she is entitled to inherit this property as H's widow. W's lawyer convinces the B judge that the A procedure of terminating a marriage without notice to the other party is contrary to the ideals of justice and fairness, and that the substance of A's divorce law—permitting an A resident to divorce a nonresident without proof of any grounds—is, when applied to B residents, contrary to B community attitudes, as reflected in B's divorce law.

Note that this hypothetical situation involves all three kinds of conflict-of-laws questions: Did State A have jurisdiction to dissolve a marriage when one party was not given an opportunity to be heard? Should State B use the legal norms of A or B to determine whether W is H's widow? Must B recognize the validity of the A divorce? While these are legal questions, how they are answered will be substantially influenced by mores and ideals.

Courts of a state in B's position are likely to lump moral considerations, together with factual considerations of public interests and values, under the rubric of public policy and thus decline to follow the legal norms of A if following A's norms would violate a strong public policy of B.

Validation of legal norms on moral grounds

Invalidation of a legally valid norm can be accomplished by showing the immorality of its substance or the way in which it was created. Validation of a legally invalid norm, the alchemy of transmuting nonlaw into law, is more complicated. Legal defects in a norm's pedigree cannot be corrected simply by showing that the procedures used to create the norm were moral (for example, approval by a fairly conducted popular vote will not validate a law requiring prescribed acts by legislative bodies). Such legal defects are overcome by showing not only that the norm's substance and the procedures followed in creating it comport with morality but also that special circumstances exist that justify overlooking the norm's pedigree in light of its substantive morality and of a strong practical need that it be treated as valid. Norms lacking legal pedigrees but with moral and factual claims for being treated as law seem to include those that are validated by a successful revolution and, more routinely, by official fiat, as when a judge engages in judicial legislation.

Validation by successful revolution

It is a truism that the only legal revolutions are those that succeed. Then "criminals" become national heroes, officials and supporters of the old regime become criminals, and subjects without previous authority to make valid law become legislators. The factual seizure of power by one group from another tends to obscure the moral complexity of a successful revolution, which involves two profound moral commitments by the revolutionaries: to break from the old allegiance (as the rebelling American colonists did in 1776 with the Declaration of Independence); and, after the old government has been deprived of physical power, to give one's allegiance to the new regime (as the founding fathers of the United States did in 1789 in adopting and implementing the U.S. Constitution).

For most people, it is morally wrong—as a matter of how they would register their opinions, of how they perceive their obligations, and of the ideals they would choose to be governed and to live by—to rebel against a government whose protection they have accepted unless that protection is withdrawn (as happened to German Jews under Hitler) or unless that government has become so evil that citizens feel morally obliged to stake their lives, property, and honor to replace it (as many Germans of all faiths felt under Hitler). In the Declaration of Independence, Thomas Jefferson and his colleagues tried to explain why they felt a moral obligation to take the illegal step of rebelling against George III. Actively rebelling against one's government is a serious step, morally and legally: allegiances calling for loyalty and obedience to the law are renounced and replaced by new allegiances in defiance of the law. And unless power is wrested from the existing government, the rebel is an outlaw, without legal rights.

If the government is ousted (as happened in the American Revolution at Yorktown with the surrender of Cornwallis in 1781) and a new government established, the people involved must then go through another, and often more difficult, moral change from being in rebellion against the old government and in defiance of its laws to being loyal to the new government and obedient to its laws. The histories of revolutions indicate that it takes a very bad and inept legitimate government to move large numbers of people to make the painful moral decision to rebel against it; and that, when enough people of the right sort at the right time make the decision to bring about the downfall of the existing government, it is then usually even more difficult to persuade enough people of the right sort to make the moral decision to give their loyalty and obedience to the new government and its norms. (Note that after the American revolutionaries had spent five years ousting the British, it took them eight more years to constitute their new government.) Only when this second moral commitment is made by enough of the state's officials and subjects to enable its legal system to function is the revolution truly successful and the norms of the new government made legally valid.

Thus, when a successful revolution occurs, the norms of a new and initially illegal legal system are validated on the nonlegal grounds of morals and facts: a circumstance that supports the theory, propounded by Kelsen, that a legal system's basic norm—the hypothesis that the system exists—can itself achieve legitimacy, and thus serve to validate the lower norms derived from it, without being legally created. Of course, when the old government does follow legal procedures and grants independence to part of its domain (as many countries have done in decolonizing their empires), the new regime has a clear legal title and there is no need to go outside the law to morals and facts in order to legitimate its legal system.

Validation by official fiat

Validation by revolution is achieved when people without official standing create new law by setting up a new legal system. Validation by official fiat is achieved when people with official standing, but without legal authority to legislate, create new law within an existing legal system. In both situations, appeals to morality and policy are substituted for observance of legal procedures, but the appeals are different in their scopes. Validation by revolution (i.e., by real revolution, as distinguished from a seizure of power that simply substitutes one ruling group for another) involves the transformation into legal norms of broad moral claims about how a state should be governed—say, with liberty, equality, and fraternity. In contrast, when judges and other officials legislate morality, they are usually legalizing some quite specific moral norms. These moral norms may come from external sources—foreign law, religious doctrine, custom, ethics—or from the officials' own consciences or ideals about justice and fairness.

While legalizations by officials of moral norms from various external sources seem less arbitrary and arouse less political opposition than do attempts to legislate personal morality, they still pose problems for theorists trying to separate law from nonlaw. Officials of one state may treat the legal norms of another state as authoritative, on moral rather than legal grounds, not only in the conflict-of-laws situations discussed above but also because the two states share a common legal tradition. At some times and places, officials have been expected to turn practically all moral norms derived from prevailing religious doctrines into valid law; and in states with established churches, ecclesiastical law often governs family relationships. In the United States, however, with its constitutional separation of church and state, judges have given religious beliefs legal standing only to the extent of protecting from governmental interference some exercises of individual religious conscience (regarding issues like military service, education of children, saluting the flag, birth control), while refusing protection for other such exercises (plural marriages, refusals of blood transfusions). Customs of particular communities or occupations—especially those relating to commerce, property rights, and employment relations—have long been a fertile, and relatively uncontroversial, field for judicial legalization of moral norms. To the extent that ethical obligations are enforceable by one's peers through the moral sanctions of censure and expulsion, legalization generally has not seemed necessary (for professionals, military officers, and members of Congress, disgrace may be punishment enough); but when moral sanctions are ineffectual or inappropriate, there is more pressure for legal sanctions (censure by or expulsion from employment by a corporation or a government may not seem to be sufficient punishment).

Controversy is more likely when officials draw not on these external moral sources (foreign laws, religious doctrines, customs, and ethical obligations) but rather on the dictates of their own consciences or their own ideals of justice and fairness. Judges and other officials who seek to convert their own morality into law risk being accused of usurping the power of the legislature. But how can they avoid resorting to their own morality when the laws they administer are incomplete or ambiguous, and objective moral sources do not resolve these legal inadequacies?

One action that officials can take is to try to separate in their own minds the issue of a norm's legal validity from the issue of its legal meaning—that is, to separate the problem of the law's incompleteness from the problem of its ambiguity. Judges are empowered to interpret the law, but they are supposed to leave lawmaking to legislators. In practice, this distinction is often elusive: the resolution of ambiguity (*this* is not due process) often seems indistinguishable from legislation (*this* is illegal). But there is a difference. Judges and other officials applying already legalized moral norms (such as due process) might use their own notions about what is and is not due process in deriving subsidiary legal norms from this moral (and legal) norm; but, in this derivation, they will be limited by the legal meaning already given to due process. For example, officials cannot (unless they are part of a majority of the Supreme Court) now derive from the due process clause—in the face of its legal history—a legal norm prohibiting a state from outlawing child labor.

Situations may arise, however, in which the law is truly incomplete, and practical need joins with morality to urge that a judge or other official be allowed to take the initiative to make a new law to fill the gap. (The rule permitting judges to refuse to enforce unconscionable contracts arose from such situations.) Here, the judge or other official must choose between legislating and permitting an unjust and costly result (and perhaps urging the legislature to act). Which way the judge or other official will go in these hard cases will depend on several factors: the size of the injustice and the cost to society in allowing it to happen; whether the gap in the law is in an area covered by statutory or decisional law; whether it is a gap purposefully left by the legislature; and whether there is a practical likelihood that the legislature will take timely corrective action.

Tension Concerning Abstract Legal Meaning

When a norm's legal meaning rather than its legal validity is in question, law and morals come into tension in a different way. Meaning, unlike validity, is not a yes-or-no issue. Although the law provides procedures for determining legal meaning, these procedures do not ensure clear-cut answers as do those for determining validity: these fix tribunals and prescribe steps for the adjudication of meaning but leave meaning itself unresolved. Lawyers tell clients, confidently and categorically, how to form valid marriages and corporations, but they are more circumspect about explaining what it means to be married or incorporated.

This section describes the kinds of law-morals tension that may arise in determining what a valid legal norm means in the abstract (as distinguished from its meaning in situations, the topic of the next section). It examines tension over deriving meaning from what a norm says, from why it was created, and from what has happened since its creation.

Tension over what a norm says

One way to begin to give meaning to the text of a legal norm is to define its terms. Law-morals tension in the definition process can arise over whether the process is to be viewed, like validity, as referring only to legal procedures and their legal consequences (to be married is to have gone through a legally prescribed ceremony and have assumed thereby legally defined obligations), or as also referring to the moral consequences of following legal procedures (to be married is to have assumed moral, as well as legal, obligations). And if legal meaning is more than following legal procedures and includes references to substantive moral norms, then tension arises over whether the law should create its own legal definitions of these norms (say, as to what is reasonable or fair or husbandly) or whether, for each legal problem, it should seek these definitions outside the law from morality. These tensions are complex because the texts of legal norms mingle conventional legal language, which is intelligible in its legal sense only within a legal system (as balls and strikes are intelligible in their baseball sense only within the game of baseball), with ordinary, more general, language, moral and factual, which is not tied to the law for its meaning.

Legal language

Legal education requires learning a new vocabulary of conventional legal terms (like *negligence, contract, malice, title, agent, corporation*), which have special legal meanings when they appear in a legal norm. But definitions of these terms often refer to moral norms (*negligence* indicates lack of due care) or are qualified by other legal norms that refer to moral norms (the meaning of the word *contract* is qualified by norms empowering judges to decline to enforce agreed-upon provisions that are unconscionable or unreasonably restrain trade). Thus, while legal language is specially defined for the legal system, and while important parts of these definitions can be treated as validity is and referred to legal procedures, it is difficult either to confine these definitions to the law or to avoid making reference to moral norms. For example, the definition of legal title to property involves compliance with legal formalities; but it is subject to the recognition of equitable title in some circumstances—largely defined by moral considerations of fairness—in which legal formalities are lacking.

Tension may arise over how the moral norms that underlie legal terms, as the norm of due care underlies negligence, are to be interpreted. Should the law create its own, peculiarly legal translations of those norms? Or should legal thinkers go outside the law in each case to moral attitudes, obligations, or ideals? Or are there other ways of giving moral meanings to legal terms?

The devices of calling certain conduct (say, the violation of a statute) "negligence per se" and certain restraints of trade (say, price-fixing agreements among competitors) "unreasonable per se" and of finding "constructive malice" when a killing occurs in the course of a felony are examples of the law creating its own legal versions of moral norms. In contrast, the legal construct of the "reasonably prudent person," often used as the norm for measuring due care, requires the law to refer moral issues directly to moral judgment on a case-by-case basis.

This tension between morals as law and morals as morals in giving meaning to legal language can take the form of disagreement over whether application of a moral norm to a legal term is a question of law for the judge to decide (the usual procedure for allegedly unconscionable contracts) or whether it is a question of fact for the jury to decide (the usual procedure for negligence). More broadly, the use of juries has been a way to resolve law-morals tension: a jury is thought to personify the moral attitudes (sometimes the prejudices) of a community but is subject to the supervision of a judge, who is thought to be better qualified to reconcile what the law requires with moral obligations and ideals.

Ordinary language, moral and factual

As the idea of distinguishing between balls and strikes has meaning only in the realm of baseball, so does the idea of distinguishing between partnerships and corporations have meaning only in the realm of law. But the norms of games and legal systems also include ideas expressed in ordinary language, moral and factual, which can refer to things both inside and outside the norms' realms. This ordinary, nonlegal moral and factual language introduces its own kind of law-morals tension into legal thinking over whether its abstract legal meaning is to be determined by legal convention or by extralegal moral judgment. The quality of this tension depends in part on whether the ordinary language is moral or factual.

Moral language. Like legal terms, moral terms express normative ideas about what ought to be done, but the "oughtness" is found in attitudes, obligations, or ideals rather than in legal convention. When moral terms are given legal status by their incorporation into legal norms, to what extent are they transformed into conventional legal terms—both procedurally, as to how their meanings are determined and substantively, as to what they mean?

For example, legal norms about homicide and constitutional rights employ moral norms to determine, respectively, when those who kill ought to be punished (when they are blameworthy) and how governments ought to treat their subjects (with due process and equal protection). Blameworthiness, also called culpability, requires a morally bad state of mind, called malice in the homicide context. Due process and equal protection require that the reasonability and evenhandedness of state action be morally justified. The law-morals tensions generated by these moral terms may be either procedural or substantive.

Procedural tension develops over whether meanings of moral terms are to be determined by legal rules or by ad hoc judgments made about the actual moral positions of those involved. Examples of legal rules used to determine meanings of moral terms are the felony-murder rule, which states that one who accidentally causes another's death while committing a felony (say robbery or rape) is guilty of murder, on the theory that the bad mind required for the felony provides the bad mind for the killing; and the Miranda rule, which states that the failure of a police officer to advise a suspect in custody of his or her rights is an automatic violation of due process, even if the advice was not needed.

Substantive tension about moral language develops when significant differences exist between judicial interpretations of moral norms—whether incorporated into legal rules or derived case by case directly from morals—and the way in which they are interpreted by others. For example, judges may be at variance with community attitudes as to whether mental disease reduces criminal blameworthiness, or whether it is reasonable for states to outlaw abortion, or whether busing of school children is an appropriate remedy for racially segregated schools. Similarly, judges may be out of step with business ethics in defining unreasonable restraints of trade or unconscionable provisions in contracts, and with professional ethics in defining conflicts of interest.

Factual language. Unlike legal and moral terms, factual terms in ordinary usage state what is, rather than what ought to be. When used in legal (and moral) norms, however, factual language takes on normative meaning, and procedural and substantive tension develops—tension similar to that with moral language in legal norms, but with the difference that factual terms have no nonlegal normative reference. Thus, the conflict is not whether a legal or an ordinary definition is to be used, but whether the factual term is to be transformed into a legal convention or is to provide an occasion for a moral judgment.

Suppose that a legal norm sets a speed limit for railroad trains while crossing "any drawbridge" over a navigable stream (as did the statute in *Savannah, F & W Ry* v. *Daniels*, decided in Georgia in 1882). Determination of the abstract legal meaning of this norm raises such questions as: Does the drawbridge consist of the whole bridge? Or does it consist only of the part over a navigable stream? Or only of the part that draws? In answering such questions about the legal meaning of factual terms in legal norms, legal thinkers have several options. They may treat a drawbridge like a partnership or a corporation and say that its legal meaning is purely a matter of legal interpretation for a judge to make, unaided by jury or expert witness, on the basis of what the lawmakers said and intended to say. Or, still keeping morals out of it, they may decide that factual terms retain their factual character in legal norms and that the ordinary meaning of a drawbridge, perhaps as defined by engineering experts, should be used to determine the term's legal meaning. Or, as often happens, they may conclude that there is no satisfactory legal or factual definition of a drawbridge for their purposes—the intent of the lawmakers is likely to be unclear and the testimony of experts to be conflicting or irrelevant. In the last case, legal thinkers proceed to make moral judgments about which legal meaning seems reasonable in the context of particular norms. And in this process they will probably find themselves thinking about the purposes and histories of the norms they are construing.

Tension over why a norm was created

What a legal norm says is there to be read and construed; uncertainty is rare about either its existence or what evidence of meaning is to be considered. In contrast, the examination of why a norm was created lacks a specific target with definite boundaries and mingles subjective perceptions with objective needs. Now the tension is not about defining words but about assigning reasons; it is not about what the legislator said but about the more complex question of what moved the legislator to legislate, which often must be pieced together from a hodgepodge of legal, moral, and political history.

The tension is now between legal and moral perspectives on why a norm was created. Those thinking from the legal perspective about the purpose of a new legal norm tend to limit its departure from existing law and to interpret its purpose narrowly in order to preserve legal continuity and predictability. And if the new legal norm introduces moral norms, they seek ways to cut through moral complexity by reducing the moral norms to legal rules or principles. Those thinking from the moral perspective, however, tend to emphasize the remedial aspects of the new legal norm and to interpret its purpose broadly in order to bring the law in line with morals—and they have scant concern about introducing moral complexity into the law. The legal perspective sees morals as gradually and incrementally reforming and improving the law, but without blurring the line between what the law does and does not permit or require. The moral perspective sees law as periodically getting radically out of step with morals and needing drastic structural change, which often means that legal clarity yields to moral ambiguity.

Chapter 3 indicated that one of the best clues to a legal norm's meaning is the "mischief" it was created to remedy: the gap in the prior law that seemed to call for a new norm. This time-honored and useful notion combines legal and moral perspectives. The gap in the law is a legal gap, but it is a mischievous legal gap because morals make it so. And, if the gap is not entirely filled by a new law, legal and moral considerations vie to measure the extent to which the gap has been closed. The illustrations of how purpose shapes meaning given in Chapter 3—using federal securities regulation, the Fourteenth Amendment, the common law negligence rule, and private transactions between friends and strangers—can now also illustrate how legal and moral perspectives on the purpose of a new legal norm may be in tension.

Securities regulation

The perceived gap in pre-1933 securities law was its failure to require those with material inside information about the value of securities to disclose this information when they sold or bought these securities. Law-morals tension arises in interpreting federal legislation enacted to do something about this gap, because the law does not ordinarily require sellers and buyers to disclose all they know (buyer—and seller—beware is the general rule of the marketplace), while moral attitudes, obligations, and ideals condemn unfair bargains. Should the purpose of the legislation be seen as a limited modification of prior law that allowed buyers and sellers to fend for themselves, or should it be seen as enactment of a new paternalistic moral code of fairness in securities transactions? Similar tension in legislative purpose—between modifying laissez-faire practices and introducing legally mandated fairness—can be found in interpretation of legal norms outlawing unreasonable restraints of trade and empowering judges to refuse to enforce unconscionable contracts. Was the purpose of these rules simply to put some specific legal constraints on market dealing, or was it to enact broad legal mandates for more equitable marketplaces?

The Fourteenth Amendment

The gap in the pre-1868 law, before the Fourteenth Amendment became part of the Constitution, was that states were permitted to restrict individual rights on the basis of race. The purpose of the Fourteenth Amendment was to provide a legal resolution to the principal moral issue of the Civil War by limiting how states can treat their subjects. Law-morals tension arises in using this purpose to interpret the amendment, because states are legally recognized as sovereign (the king can do no wrong), but the way in which some states were treating some of those subject to their power was morally recognized as wrong by the side that prevailed in the Civil War. Should the purpose of the Fourteenth Amendment be regarded as a limited modification of state sovereignty or as the legalization of a new moral code of individual rights? (Actually, for about seventy years after 1868, state sovereignty remained virtually intact as against individuals but was considerably reduced as against business enterprises. Since the 1930s, the positions of individuals and business enterprises have been effectively reversed.)

Negligence

The gap in Anglo-American tort law prior to the common law negligence rule, developed by English and American judges in the first half of the twentieth century, was the absence of a broad principle for allocating the economic cost of accidents. Law-morals tension arises in interpreting the negligence rule because of differences between legal and moral perspectives of the rule's purpose. The legal perspective sees this purpose as the assignment of liability on the basis of fault, however pardonable the lapse or remote its consequences. While ostensibly legalizing the moral norm that one should exercise due care, this legal perspective is nevertheless at odds with the moral perspective. The latter does not see the purpose of the rule as imposition of automatic liability upon "negligent" defendants for remote, unforeseeable consequences of their mildly careless conduct; rather, the moral perspective calls for more complex moral judgments—moral because they focus on fairness rather than on legal fault—about the foreseeability of consequences, the magnitude of the carelessness, the comparative fault of the parties, and their relative ability to pass on the cost of the accident.

Private transactions

The gap in the law before two subjects conclude a private transaction is that neither is legally obligated to the other. If they are friends, their views of the transaction and its purpose may be preponderantly moral: they may feel that as friends they are already morally obligated to treat each other fairly and that the imposition of legal obligation is superfluous, even repugnant, to their friendship. But if they are strangers, their views of the transaction and its purpose will be in the context of legal obligations, and there will seem to be little occasion for morals to enter the picture, although each would probably resent being treated unfairly by the other.

To summarize, it appears that the legal perspective regarding the purpose of a new legal norm focuses less on the mischief that occasioned its creation than on the actual legal remedy that was created to deal with the mischief, and that this perspective is likely to assume that a definable part of the mischief was meant to be dealt with. This perspective's bias is toward preserving the rigor, clarity, and dignity of the law by avoiding major changes in existing law, by resisting the introduction of uncertainty and moral ambiguity, and by emphasizing the following of legal forms. The moral perspective on legislative purpose, however, focuses on the gap in the existing law that caused the new norm to be created and tends to assume that the new norm was meant to deal with all of the mischief resulting from the gap. The moral perspective's bias favors broad change and keeping the law in step with morals; this perspective is little concerned with legal continuity, certainty, or formality. In short, the legal perspective, less confident than the moral perspective about what is right, is more willing to settle for clarity about what is legal.

Tension over what has happened since the norm was created

To learn what a legal norm means when it is made, we read its text and seek its purpose. But events can change meaning. These happenings can be within a legal system, as when the norm is applied to new and different events; and they may be in the world at large. In addition, as with a norm's text and purpose, the impact of new circumstances on meaning can be viewed from legal and moral perspectives. The legal perspective assumes that legal meaning changes only when officials authoritatively recognize new legal meaning. The moral perspective assumes that legal meaning changes when moral meaning changes. Tension between these perspectives is apparent in the twentieth-century transformations, noted in Chapter 3, in the concepts of due care and due process, both areas in which the law had lagged in reflecting changes in predominant moral notions.

Of course, moral meaning is not monolithic. At any one time, moral attitudes, obligations, and ideals may themselves be at odds. As happened with racial segregation under the equal protection clause, a legal principle may be given new meaning on the strength of change in a legally accepted moral ideal, while the moral attitudes of many continue to countenance the status quo. (In that instance, the Supreme Court made the change in legal principle by abandoning the rationale that separate but equal facilities provide equal protection of the law.) And, as the history of desegregation demonstrates, judges expose themselves to political risks when they espouse moral ideals or seek to impose on other officials moral obligations that are at odds with widely and strongly held moral attitudes.

To illustrate the imponderable choices, for judges and other legal thinkers, in determining whether legal meaning changes with moral change or only when this change is given legal recognition, consider the legal status of abortion. Changes outside the law—notably, growth in the number, safety, and respectability of abortions—plus some changes within the law reflecting these events have generated strongly held and widely disparate views about what is morally right for the many parties involved, and what their legal rights are. These parties include pregnant women, their doctors, their conceived but unborn children, the state, and others with interests in women and their fetuses. Legal norms involved in this controversy (and some of the questions raised about their meanings) include constitutional norms about individual liberty and the power of the state to interfere with it through criminal laws (Does a woman have a right to decide what happens to her body? Does her doctor have a right to help her make and implement her decision? Correlatively, does a state have the power to enact criminal laws that interfere with her decision?) and family law norms about the legal claims of others involved (What are the rights, if any, of a woman's husband, her unborn child's natural father, and, if she is unemancipated (under 18 and unmarried), her parents or guardian, to prevent or insist on an abortion?).

Suppose (as matters of law) that a fetus is not recognized as a legal person, with the result that abortion is not considered murder or homicide, but that some abortions can be made criminal; and that an emancipated woman and her doctor have a legal right, free of interference by the state or anyone else, to decide whether to abort a fetus during the first three months of a pregnancy. Suppose further (as matters of fact) that hundreds of thousands of abortions are performed in the United States each year and that, while abortions are more respectable than they used to be, most of the population purports to hold the following moral attitudes: that at some time before birth a fetus becomes a person whom it is wrong to kill; that women and their doctors do not have an unqualified moral right to bring about abortions; that in some situations natural fathers have a moral right to veto decisions to abort, including some of those made during the first three months of pregnancy; and that the state has a moral power to criminalize some abortions. With these assumptions, conflicts between existing legal norms and moral attitudes are narrow but crucial:

- Legal norms say that abortion cannot be homicide and that during the first three months of pregnancy emancipated women and their doctors have an unqualified right to abort.
- Moral attitudes say that abortion can be wrongful killing and that natural fathers and the state should be able to limit, through civil and criminal proceedings, the right of women (including those who are emancipated) and their doctors to bring about abortions, even during the first three months of pregnancy.

The above discussion, which limits its assumptions about morals to the attitudes of the majority, might be quite different if assumptions were also hazarded about the dictates of conscience and ideals. Many whose professed attitudes are antiabortion might find it in their consciences to approve of abortions for themselves or those close to them. Nonetheless, many who would recognize a right to abortion as an ideal of justice or fairness might find abortion repugnant to their consciences for themselves or those close to them. And these seemingly opposing groups might be able to unite on keeping abortion in the preserve of individual moral judgment and on making the only legal norm the constitutional norm that there shall be no other legal norms that speak to this issue. While this position abdicates to morals the substantive issue of the rightness and wrongness of an abortion, it does so by adopting the legal perspective of how changes in moral meaning affect legal meaning: that moral meaning becomes legal meaning only when the law recognizes it as such.

Tension Concerning Situational Legal Meaning and Whether Legal Norms Should be Applied to Events

This section introduces the new elements of a factual event, calling for a situational (but still, of course, normative), as distinguished from abstract, meaning for a legal norm, and the need for a determination of whether the norm should be applied to the event. Something happens in the world outside the legal system—a barroom fight, a highway accident, a business conversation—triggering conceptualization of a legal situation in the mind of a legal thinker. Whatever his or her point of view, the thinker puts together the facts of the event and the abstract meaning of the pertinent legal norm—about assault and battery (or homicide), negligence, contracts—plus other seemingly relevant circumstances and pertinent normative materials to construct a concept (a legal situation) about how event and norm connect with each other. Among other things, this concept transforms the norm's abstract meaning into a situational meaning in preparation for determining whether the norm ought to be applied to the event. At both of these stages—constructing the norm's situational meaning and then determining whether the norm should rule the event—law-morals tension arises, but in different ways. This distinction, created by law-morals tension, between what a norm means and whether it ought to be applied to an event, was not considered in Chapter 3's introductory discussion regarding the applicability stage of a legal problem.

Tension in constructing the situational meaning of legal norms

For each thinker, a legal norm has only one abstract meaning at a time but as many situational meanings as there are situations of which it is a part. Abstract meaning is a product of a norm's text, purpose, and history. Situational meaning is a product of the fit between abstract meaning and an event. Tension arises between law and morals in making this fit. The tension can be about fitting both the norm to the event and the event to the norm—that is, about how abstract meaning of the norm is particularized to determine whether it is pertinent to the event, and about how details of the event and its circumstances are selected and interpreted to determine whether they are relevant to the norm. Particularizing the norm creates smaller legal categories (more specific legal meaning); selecting relevant facts creates more focused accounts of events (less irrelevant detail).

Concerning both the pertinence of norms to facts and the relevance of facts to norms, the law-morals tension typically is between what seems logical and what seems morally right. In theory, the legal approach to constructing situational meaning permits no judgments other than logical ones about how to tailor abstract meaning to the event at hand or how to organize facts in light of categories furnished by abstract meaning; and the legal approach is supposed to be disinterested regarding results. The moral approach, on the other hand, calls for judgments about the morality both of how the norm-event fit is determined and of the fit itself.

To illustrate law-morals tension in making the norm-event fit in constructing situational meaning, consider the 1931 case (*McBoyle* v. *United States*) in which the Supreme Court decided that an airplane is not a motor vehicle—a favorite with law teachers trying to explain situational meaning because the law and the facts are simple and the opinion was written by Justice Holmes (in his ninetieth year). In 1919, when car theft was replacing horse stealing, Congress enacted the National Motor Theft Act, making it a federal offense to transport in interstate commerce "a motor vehicle, knowing the same to have been stolen," and providing: "The term *'motor vehicle' shall include an automobile,* automobile truck, motor cycle, *or any other self-propelled vehicle not designed for running on rails*" (emphasis added). In reversing a conviction under this act for transporting an airplane known to have been stolen, Holmes said that, while the meaning of the word *vehicle* is "etymologically" (by which he apparently meant "according to the dictionary") broad enough to be used "to signify a conveyance working on land, water or air, . . . in every-day speech 'vehicle' calls up the picture of a thing moving on land," and that therefore it would not be fair to hold the act applicable to an airplane. Holmes particularized the norm to create a smaller legal category that has no room for conveyances that do not move on land, which led him to select as most relevant the factual detail about airplanes that they travel mainly in the air, instead of, for example, the fact that they are self-propelled.

Note that using the broad, dictionary meaning of vehicle, the letter of the law seems logically to cover a stolen airplane. And Holmes concedes for the sake of argument that a similar policy may apply to stolen automobiles and airplanes and that, if Congress had thought of it, "very likely broader words would have been used." Nevertheless, he seems to conclude that to interpret the statute literally would be morally wrong, both as to the method followed (because, in his words, it is at variance with what the words of the statute "evoke in the common mind") and as to the result achieved (because, as he put it, it fails to give "fair warning . . . to the world in language that the common world will understand of what the law intends to do if a certain line is passed").

Later generations of lawyers and their clients may wonder what has happened to this respect for everyday speech. And is it either practicable or just to leave legal meaning to judicial speculation about "the common mind"? Although the word *vehicle* is used in the National Motor Theft Act as a conventional legal term with a legally defined meaning, Holmes treated it as a term of everyday speech, with its legal meaning, abstract and situational, subject to the vagaries of what judges perceive to be going on in something he called the common mind. (In Holmes's defense, however, it should be noted that he also argued from the text that Congress must have been using *vehicle* in the popular sense, because its use of the word *running* in its definition of vehicle shows that its theme was a vehicle running on land.)

Tension in determining whether a legal norm should be applied to an event

Even after a legal norm's situational meaning has been constructed and any law-morals tension concerning that process or result has been resolved, tension is still possible concerning whether the norm's legal "ought" or some moral "ought" from outside the law is to determine whether the norm should be applied to the event. The force of logic may be so ineluctable regarding the content of the norm's abstract meaning and its fit with the event that the legal thinker seems to have no choice but to conclude that the norm ought, or ought not, to be applied to the event. At the same time, however, the thinker may be convinced that it would be profoundly wrong, because of moral considerations, to reach this conclusion. Variations of this dilemma, which pits a clear legal meaning against a strong moral imperative, run through literature and life: it was experienced by Abraham when he was ordered to sacrifice his son, by Antigone when she was forbidden to bury her brother, by officials of the Third Reich who were ordered to enforce immoral laws.

A case much favored by legal philosophers to illustrate tension between situational legal meaning and morals involves whether Elmer Palmer, having been convicted of murdering his grandfather to prevent him from changing a will that made Elmer his principal beneficiary, should now be permitted to receive the legacy under the will (*Riggs* v. *Palmer*, decided in New York in 1889). The question confronting the court was: Should it refuse to give legal effect to a duly made and probated will that constituted a valid, unambiguous legal norm about the devolution of property, and the situational meaning of which contained no exception for a legatee who is a murderer? If Elmer had murdered someone else, this circumstance would not disqualify him as a legatee, because the law no longer strips felons of their property. Should it make a difference that the murder was done to ensure the legacy? The court could find no American or English statute or case that so held (although the Napoleonic Code contains a provision to this effect). Nevertheless, the court denied Elmer his legacy, using as justification the general principle of equity that no one should be permitted to profit from his own wrong and declaring that a contrary holding "would be a reproach to the jurisprudence of our state, and an offense against public policy."

Another case, sometimes used in tandem with the *Palmer* case, is *Henningsen* v. *Bloomfield Motors*, decided in New Jersey in 1960, in which the written purchase contract for a new automobile limited the manufacturer's liability to replacing defective parts and excluded any implied warranties. The buyer of a defective car, unable to prove that the manufacturer had been negligent, asserted an implied warranty. Thus, as in the *Palmer* case, a court had to decide whether the clear legal meaning of a legal norm (in this case a contract that specified that no warranties were to be implied) or something else was to govern the norm's applicability in this situation. The New Jersey court decided that, notwithstanding the importance of the freedom to contract, this freedom is not absolute, and that a court may withhold enforcement of contractual provisions it finds to be unjust, even though these provisions are otherwise valid, unambiguous, and pertinent in the situation; and, as to the waiver of implied warranties, the court concluded that, in the purchase of a product as necessary and dangerous as an automobile, "an instinctively felt sense of justice cries out against such a sharp bargain."

These two cases raise the troublesome question of whether the New York and New Jersey courts were acting judicially or legislatively—of whether, in determining whether legal norms ought to be applied to events, they were using legal meaning or were making new law based on morals. In other words, were the arguments they used in these cases to justify their decisions—not allowing profit from one's own wrong, and not enforcing sharp bargains—based on legal principles or on their perceptions of morality? If the justifications can be called legal, as some commentators have argued, then the law-morals tension disappears and the judges are absolved of charges that they are legislating or indulging in judicial activism. But it is difficult to see what makes these justifications legal. In neither case does the court rely on statute or precedent, or even on custom; rather, the courts refer to "public policy" and the "sense of justice." To call these factual or moral considerations legal, it seems necessary to view the law as lacking boundaries—as encompassing what judges think it should encompass—and to abandon the effort, to which this chapter has been directed, to draw a line between law and morals.

Perhaps it is possible both to preserve the law-morals distinction and to permit morals to enter thinking about legal problems by introducing moral considerations before a legal problem has reached its final normative stage—that is, at the stages of validity, abstract meaning, or situational meaning, rather than at the stage of determining whether a legal norm ought to be applied to an event. When thinkers, particularly judges, bow to morals at this late stage, they often seem to be rejecting clear legal norms in favor of less clear moral norms derived from their own perceptions of community attitudes or from what they find in their own consciences or in the moral ideals they espouse. In contrast, yieldings of the law to morals seem less legislative and more interpretive, and thus less threatening to the law's integrity, when a legal norm's validity or meaning, abstract or situational, is unclear.

Chapter Six

TENSION BETWEEN NORMS AND FACTS

When a person determines whether or not to be guided by a valid, meaningful, normatively applicable legal norm, the tension felt is that between the authority of the norm and a prudential concern for probable consequences and their impacts on particular interests and values. This norm-fact tension about the actual application—as distinguished from the applicability discussed in the final part of the previous chapter—of norms to events arises most typically after legal situations have been conceptualized and after any law-morals tension has been resolved. Norm-fact tension is experienced directly by subjects, who must choose whether to conform their conduct to the norms, and by officials, who must decide whether the norms will govern the situations. But other legal thinkers—advisers advising subjects and officials, legislators determining whether they will make new norms, and legal scholars trying to explain how a legal system works—deal from the sidelines with other kinds of norm-fact tension. This chapter examines the contending forces creating norm-fact tension and the several points of view for experiencing this tension.

Contending Forces Creating Norm-Fact Tension

Having developed the steps in situational legal thinking that lead up to the application of a legal norm to an event, I will now focus on the thinking that determines whether or not to take this final step. This section examines two kinds of forces that compete to influence this thinking: one's respect for normative authority and one's own judgment about what is prudent.

The competing pulls of authority and prudence are not symmetrical. Authority can only provide reasons for the application of norms, whereas prudence can provide reasons for either application or nonapplication. A motorist on a slippery road has both normative and prudential reasons for obeying the speed limits, but prudence can also urge disobedience: the motorist's prudential concerns (say to be on time for an important meeting) may provide reasons for speed that are more compelling than are considerations of safety. Although norm-fact tension is most apparent when factual reasons point to not applying the norm, it is sometimes important to distinguish between applying a norm because it is the law and acting consistently with a norm for factual reasons. For example, one might refuse to obey a law requiring a formal oath about religious or political beliefs but be willing to make a voluntary statement about these beliefs. And one who obeys the law because it is prudent to do so, not because it is the law, may find it hard to be law abiding when the promptings of prudence are lacking, and even harder when they point toward disobedience.

Respect for normative authority

Much of this book has been about normativeness: the quality of saying what ought to be, as distinguished from what is. But the idea of a norm's authority, its right and power to command what ought to be, has remained relatively unanalyzed. While authority involves power, which is factual, as well as right, which is legal and moral, the power part of authority serves the right part, as its military and police forces serve a legitimate government. This subsection considers a norm's authority as evidenced by the legitimacy of the norm's origin, the moral weight of its contents, and its efficacy in obtaining respect and compliance. In short, the predominantly legal, moral, and factual aspects of normative authority are examined here.

Legal authority: The legitimacy of a norm's origin

The legal authority of a norm can be distinguished from its legal validity (its formal status as law), as well as from its moral weight and factual efficacy, by the emphasis that legal authority places on how the norm originated. A norm can be legally valid but possess dubious legal authority. In addition, a norm may have impeccable legal authority but carry little moral weight or be factually ineffective: one can acknowledge the legal authority of a speed limit, based on the legitimacy of its origin, but perceive it as having but slight moral weight and obey it only when moved by extraneous factual reasons such as the weather, a wish to be leisurely, or the presence of a police officer. If a norm lacks legal validity, the question of its legal authority does not arise, because it is not a legal norm; but a legally unauthoritative norm can be valid and have moral or factual authority; and a valid legal norm that lacks any authority—legal, moral, or factual—will probably, notwithstanding its legal validity, be disregarded in favor of some of the prudential considerations discussed in the next subsection.

The legitimacy of a norm's origin as a basis for its legal authority is less an all-or-nothing quality—and is less intensely "legal"—than is its legal validity. Consider the following examples:

- A unanimous (nine to zero) decision of the Supreme Court has no more formal validity than a split decision does, but it often has more legal (as well as moral and factual) authority. A split decision (even when the split is eight to one), especially when there is a strong minority opinion justifying a contrary result, will command less judicial respect in subsequent cases than will a unanimous decision; and the temptation will be greater for subjects (and even for officials) and their advisers to disregard the split decision in the hope that it will be reversed, especially when the split is close (five to four) or fairly close (six to three).

- While seals on documents no longer work their old-time magic, observing formalities in creating legal norms still enhances their legal authority. Property and contract rights are more secure if the documents creating them are in order; and, even in jurisdictions that recognize common law marriages or de facto corporations, ceremonial marriages or de jure corporations usually command more legal authority.
- A government coming to power by revolution or military coup is considered valid while it remains in power, but the illegitimacy of its origin may, especially in its early years, diminish the legal authority of its laws compared with those of a government coming to power by legal succession (suggesting that the distinction between validity and authority seems to hold for the basic and constitutional norms under which governments govern as well as for the lower-order norms of a legal system).

Legitimacy of normative origin depends on the legal procedures followed by the lawmaker, on the means used to create a norm. Validity, however, depends on the lawmaker having the factual power to create a norm. An operative legal norm created informally by judicial legislation or by some other exercise of official discretion (say, a rule of thumb that motorists will not be ticketed unless they exceed a speed limit by *x* miles per hour) is as valid as a duly enacted statute but is less legitimate: the informal norm's legal authority is more subject to challenge and change. And this emphasis on a norm's pedigree, rather than on its content or its efficacy, also distinguishes a norm's legal authority from its moral and factual authority.

Moral authority: The moral weight of a norm's content

Norms with equally legitimate origins have equal legal authority, without regard to the relative triviality or importance of what they command. A norm regulating where one may park one's car can possess as much legal authority as does a norm regulating when one may kill another person. The obvious difference in the normative authority of laws about parking and killing is to be found not in the legal authority of their pedigrees but in the moral authority of their contents.

In the norm-fact tension felt in applying norm to event, the clout that a norm derives from its moral authority varies with the seriousness or weight of its moral message, abstract and situational. Different norms carry different abstract moral weights: parking and killing are widely separated in our cultural spectrum of moral seriousness. Moral problems, like legal problems, can be abstract or situational, and the moral weights of norms in situations may be more or less than their abstract weights: the moral gap between parking and killing narrows when the illegally parked car blocks a fire lane or when the killing seems necessary, merciful, or accidental.

The moral weights of legal norms also vary with the moral origins of their messages to particular legal thinkers. As indicated in Chapter 2, morals may originate in community attitudes, in individual obligations of ethics and conscience, and in general ideals of justice and fairness. Normative authority based on the happenstance of current community attitudes or the quirks of individual conscience may be a less weighty counterpoise to considerations of factual prudence than the more lasting moral authority of ethical obligations or ideals of justice and fairness. And different kinds of moral origins support different kinds of norms in different ways. It seems almost absurd to say one should not kill or steal because it would be unethical or unidealistic to do so; ethics and ideals are appropriate for more subtle, less emotionally charged moral questions, such as whether one should keep one's promises or tell the truth. It seems equally absurd to say that one should be guided by community attitudes about promise keeping and truth telling, moral questions about which the prevailing attitude may be, at best, apathy. But it does not seem absurd to say that conscience keeps one from killing and stealing and, on occasion, from breaking promises and lying, because conscience seems capable of both elemental and subtle moral responses.

Assessing the weight of a legal norm's moral authority is an imprecise but important part of legal thinking. It is imprecise because it involves feelings as well as logical reasons and because it lacks procedures and officials for stating its messages and identifying their origins comparable with the procedures and officialdom available to clarify and authenticate legal authority. But the emotional and unbounded qualities of moral authority also contribute to its force; and legal authority unbuttressed by moral authority of some sort is likely to offer only feeble resistance to the persuasiveness of prudence.

Factual authority: The efficacy of a norm's command

A norm may be of doubtful legitimacy because of its procedural origin and it may be of scant moral weight because of its content, but it may still possess normative authority because subjects and officials respond to it as a binding norm. An example is the judicially legislated rule of contributory negligence, still the law in many states despite its questionable fairness. (It states that if both parties to an accident are negligent, neither can recover from the other, even if one is much less at fault than the other.) Conversely, a norm may have an unquestionably legitimate origin and a clearly moral content and in fact lack normative authority because subjects and officials do not respond to it as a binding norm. A familiar example is the duly legislated and reasonable speed limit that is generally disregarded by subjects and officials alike. These examples indicate that normative authority includes, independent of a norm's legitimacy or morality, a factual component that depends on the norm's efficacy in terms of the response it evokes from subjects and officials. And this normative efficacy is also different from factual considerations of prudence, the topic of the next subsection, in that the norm is still regarded, or disregarded, as a norm. Judges and lawyers apply the contributory negligence rule because it is the law, not because they think it prudent to do so. And, while prudence may color the responses of subjects and officials to a reasonable speed limit, disregard of this norm may have nothing to do with balancing normative authority against factual prudence: the norm may simply be treated as though it has no normative authority.

The facts involved in the factual authority of a legal norm are neither social facts about community attitudes nor predictions about what will happen if a norm is applied or not applied. Rather, they are facts about whether the norm is binding, about how people respond to it. Determining the efficacy of a norm's command provokes such questions as:

- Does the norm have a history of being responded to as a binding law? For example, where the contributory negligence rule has not been legislatively or judicially replaced by some other rule, it is responded to as law. In contrast, many speed limits, along with many other laws formally in effect in legal systems everywhere, are treated as dead letters.
- Does the substance of the norm conflict with current priorities? Laws aimed at protecting the environment lose efficacy when energy is scarce and the economy in trouble. In contrast, laws regulating immigration seem to become more binding when unemployment rises, and the normative authority of a draft registration law increases as the perceived need for armed forces increases.
- Is the norm regarded as capable of solving anything? Laws regulating various forms of "vice"—prostitution, homosexuality, gambling, the sale of alcoholic beverages—may not seem worth trying to enforce. But enforcement may seem worth the effort with laws regulating the sale and possession of items regarded as dangerous, such as drugs and weapons, and with laws enhancing the quality of life, such as those regulating highway billboards.

While some of these questions—about a norm's history, relevance, and usefulness—involve community attitudes as well as consequences to interests and values, they do so not to discover moral meaning or make prudential judgments but rather to assess the normative power of a particular norm. As noted before, normative authority is the right and power to command what ought to be. Normative right is a question of law and morals. Normative power is a question of fact, but it is a question of fact about normativeness: it considers questions such as whether a law actually (as a fact) has been duly (according to a norm) enacted and whether the content of a norm reflects the moral dictates of attitudes, obligations, or ideals.

In order to assess the normative authority of a valid, meaningful, normatively applicable legal norm, a legal thinker thinks not only about the legitimacy of its origin and the moral weight of its content but also about its factual power to command the response of subjects and officials. If he or she finds that it lacks such power (say, because it is a dead letter), the thinker may opt to stop there and simply not apply the norm; or if he or she finds its normative power irresistible (say, because the thinker is an official and the norm is a rule of long standing), he or she may opt to stop there and simply apply the norm. But, if the legal thinker does not stop there, his or her conclusions about the norm's legal and moral right and factual power will be but the first part of the thinking. The next part will be to give attention to whether it is prudent to let the authority of the norm determine the outcome of the thinker's problem.

Judgments about what is prudent

Normative authority never tells one not to apply an applicable norm; it simply tells (or fails to tell) one to apply the norm. And the norm's legal status suffices to justify, and largely to define, its authority. The message of prudence is more complicated: it may urge that an applicable norm be applied or not applied; and there are no ready-made limits on how far afield it may go in its projections and assessments.

Chapter 3 explained how objective data about events and their circumstances—data about fights, accidents, transactions—trigger conceptualizations of legal situations that connect facts with norms in one's mind. In this process, facts passively wait to be discovered and fitted to norms. But, at the action stage of legal thinking, when norms are actually applied (or not applied), facts may be assertive. They may compete with norms by urging on the thinker prudential, rather than normative, reasons for acting or thinking in a certain way. These reasons are the facts described in Chapter 2 as subjective judgments of prudence about consequences and their impact on interests and values. When one ponders whether to be ruled by a valid, unambiguous, normatively applicable rule (say, a speed limit), the tension in the thinker's mind is not between the authority of the rule and the objective event and its circumstances (weather, traffic, road conditions, light, presence or absence of officials), but between the authority of the rule and the thinker's subjective judgments about what is likely to happen if the rule is applied or not applied and about how these consequences may affect the thinker's interests or values.

The voice of normative authority asks no determination of the thinker other than the ultimate determination to be a law-abiding person. Although the voice of prudence can speak loudly and clearly (when, for example, applying the law will almost certainly cause or avert a great loss), seeking the guidance of prudence usually means making a series of less than ultimate determinations. First, one makes forecasts of alternate futures, a process that entails choosing and applying the relevant data and the forecasting method; then one selects among the forecasts, a process that entails selecting and using standards for favoring one future over another. The following discussion of consequences deals with making the forecasts; the subsequent discussions of interests and values deal with selecting among the forecasts.

Consequences

In declaring what ought to happen, norms of a normative system (a moral philosophy, a legal system, a game) share a two-way relationship in which higher norms validate lower norms and lower norms make higher norms more specific (as the law of contracts both validates and is particularized by individual contracts). Facts, however, share a different kind of two-way relationship, one based on cause and effect, since they are concerned with what is rather than what ought to be—and thus are less obviously component parts of a single system. Working from an event forward in time to its probable effect, a thinker predicts what is likely to happen (a meteorologist predicts the effect of atmospheric conditions in the West on weather in the East; a securities analyst predicts the effect of a political event on the stock market), and, working from an effect backward in time to its probable cause, a thinker deduces what is likely to have been (Sherlock Holmes, to Dr. Watson's amazement, deduces that the person with freshly muddied shoes has been recently outdoors).

While we talk about physical and social consequences both prospectively to predict results and retrospectively to deduce causes, it is in the prospective mode that consequences contend with norms. Deducing what is likely to have been is relevant in deciding whether to apply a norm only to the extent that it helps to decide whether the norm is normatively applicable to the event (Is it likely that A killed B?)—a decision now assumed already to have been made—or to the extent that it helps to predict what is likely to be (Is a jury likely to convict A of murdering B?). Past experience with law enforcement officials may influence a subject's decision about whether to obey a legal rule, but it does so because it facilitates predicting the consequences of current obedience or disobedience. Unlike the questions of physical and social scientists bent on explaining why things happen as they do (Why did the Nile flood each year? Why can't Johnny read?), the cause-and-effect question of a subject or official is: What is likely to happen if I apply or do not apply this norm in this situation? Thus, the problem is not law and morals versus the physical and social sciences, but, much more narrowly, respect for normative authority versus concern for factual consequences: the tension felt by a legal thinker between being law abiding and being prudent.

In conceptualizing the alternate futures of doing and not doing as a legal norm directs, a legal thinker makes predictions about two kinds of consequences relevant to his or her problem: direct, cause-and-effect consequences that may happen without human intervention (if I disobey a seat-belt rule, I may get hurt) and reactive consequences that depend on how other people react (if I break a contract, the other party may sue me and officials may order me to perform or pay damages for my nonperformance).

Direct consequences seem more predictable than do reactive consequences, and thinkers are less likely to seek the help of advisers in predicting them. A party to a disadvantageous contract knows the direct results of performance and nonperformance—suffering and avoiding a loss—but often needs a lawyer's help in predicting how the other party and officials are likely to react if he or she does not perform. Predicting direct consequences seems like a scientific exercise in cause-and-effect reasoning, whereas predicting reactive consequences often seems like psychological guesswork. (Suppose, for example, that among the rules I live by are avoiding green peppers and being on time for appointments. If I flout my green-pepper rule, I can confidently predict an upset stomach; but I am less confident of what the consequences will be when I am late for an appointment, because what may happen depends on the reactions of others.)

Reactive consequences include the reactions not only of other parties to an event but also of officials and of the general public. Reactions of other parties to the event frequently determine whether the machinery of the legal system will be put in motion, whether someone other than the thinker is likely to seek to have the norm applied to the event. (Even in criminal cases, police often act only on the complaints of aggrieved parties.) Reactions of officials determine whether the law will in fact bestir itself to cause the norm to be applied to the event. (Justice Holmes said, "The prophecies of what the courts will do in fact, and nothing more pretentious, are what I mean by the law.") And reactions of the general public affect not only the reputation of the legal thinker but also the authority of the norm involved and the system of which it is a part: a scofflaw denigrates him- or herself and the legal system as well as the particular law.

Frequently, consequences that favor not following a norm are those that result directly from ignoring the norm's impediments—such as continuing one's journey by ignoring a red traffic light, or not performing a contract that has become onerous, or being able more effectively to prepare a criminal case against a suspect whose constitutional rights have been slighted. In contrast, consequences that favor following a norm are likely to be reactive: the risk of being arrested for running a red light, or sued for breaking a contract, or having evidence excluded or convictions overturned because of constitutional improprieties. In addition, the conscientious will be led to follow norms by the prospect that, if they do not, they will be labeled lawbreakers who impair the authority of the law. While some direct consequences favor obedience (such as seeing oneself as law abiding and avoiding physical risks created by disobedience), it is difficult to conjure up reactive consequences that favor disobedience—although perhaps some results-oriented persons, contemptuous of normative authority, welcome being thought of as above or outside the law in order to instill fear in others.

These illustrations suggest that predictions of the consequences of applying legal norms are made not as ends in themselves—as astronomers predict lunar eclipses—but rather as preludes to making prudential judgments about the impacts of consequences on the thinker's interests or values.

Interests

For the purposes of this discussion, interests are the utilitarian needs and advantages of particular persons or groups. Thinking about consequences, a process that calls for forecasts, often merges imperceptibly into thinking about interests, a process that calls for forecasts of consequences plus calculations of their costs and benefits; and the reliability of both processes often can be enhanced by the help of advisers. But consequences and interests differ significantly. Consequences happen "out there" in the objective world of events and are not tied to particular persons or groups. Interests, while less subjective than values (because interests tell us what is useful rather than what is wanted), are more subjective than consequences: being the self-interests of particular persons or groups, interests (as the term is used here) are calculated in light of what is useful to them and to them alone.

In balancing the normative authority of an applicable legal norm against factual judgments of prudence, a legal thinker ordinarily forecasts the consequences of applying and not applying the norm in a situation in order to judge how particular interests, held by the thinker or by those he or she represents, will fare. In making this judgment, a thinker considers which abstract interests of the interest holder may be affected and what their importance to the holder is, a process roughly comparable with determining a norm's abstract meaning and authority. A thinker also thinks about how these abstract interests may be situationally affected—in terms of the magnitude, probability, timing, and measurability of anticipated costs and benefits—and about the interest holder's reaction to these impacts, a process comparable, even more roughly, with determining a norm's situational meaning. Thus, in thinking about interests, one can ask a series of connected questions:

- What is likely to happen if a norm is applied? Not applied?
- What abstract interests of the holder are likely to be affected by these happenings?
- How important to the holder are these interests?
- What are the impacts on these interests of applying the norm? Of not applying the norm?
- How important to the holder are these impacts?

The abstract interests of particular persons and groups, beyond the basic interest of survival, generally are determined primarily by the interest holders' political, economic, cultural, and religious positions and involvements in society—that is, by their possession or lack of power, property, education, and commitment. The interests of those who are powerful, propertied, educated, and involved in culture and religion are more numerous and better defined than are the interests of those who lack these endowments. The kinds of abstract interests implicated by legal problems typically involve money and other property, bodily well-being, and political freedom (and its converse, political power). These interests take many forms. For example, application and nonapplication of laws prohibiting "subversive" and "obscene" publications affect the political freedom and power, the incomes and property, the artistic self-expression and aesthetic enjoyment, the religious and moral beliefs, and even the bodily health of many persons and groups, who assign different priorities to these various interests. Abstract interests seem to be objective to the extent that they can be deduced from one's positions and involvements in society but seem to be subjective in the way they are ordered in the mind. For example, people with similar economic, cultural, and religious backgrounds may hold widely different views about the relative importance of enjoying political freedom and wielding political power.

Like interests in the abstract, impacts on abstract interests of the consequences of applying or not applying legal norms in particular situations have both objective aspects that depend on the nature of the costs and benefits to the interest holders and subjective aspects that depend on the interest holders' reactions to the cost and benefit calculations. Objective impacts can be assessed on several scales, including the following:

- Magnitude—How seriously will the abstract interest be affected? Overwhelmingly (being subjected to the death penalty, being forced into bankruptcy)? Substantially (performing a burdensome but less than disastrous contract)? Minimally (observing a speed limit and hence being late for an appointment)?
- Probability—What is the likelihood that the costs or benefits will be realized? Almost certain (being punished for failing to obey a police officer)? Highly probable (being punished for not paying one's taxes)? More likely than not (being sued for not performing a contract, or being well regarded for performing a contract)? Unlikely (being punished for not obeying a traffic signal in the absence of a police officer)?
- Timing—When will the impact be felt? Immediately (performing a burdensome contract)? Soon (observing a speed limit and hence being late for an appointment)? In the remote future (being subjected to the death penalty)?
- Measurability—To what extent can costs and benefits be quantified? With specificity (performing a contract, paying a tax, committing an offense punishable by death)? Only in general terms (obeying a censorship law)?

Costs and benefits are difficult to ignore when they are substantial, highly probable, immediate, and measurable in dollars, years, or lives. They are less pressing when they are minimal, unlikely, remote, or not measurable. And note that the illustrative impacts that came to my mind when I wrote this were almost all costs rather than benefits—an indication that negative impacts on interests seem to count more (for me) than do positive ones.

Once the objective nature of the impacts of consequences on interests—the ascertainable costs and advantages—is assessed, the question becomes the subjective one of whether these impacts are important enough to the interest holders to determine how they will act. In making this judgment, the interest holders or their representatives may have to choose between the attention they give to different impacts on the same interests: performing a burdensome contract may involve certain, immediate, exactly measurable economic costs, while repudiating the contract may risk economic costs that are less certain and more remote (the other party may not sue, or at least not right away) but are possibly of greater magnitude. And sometimes the choice is between impacts on different kinds of interests: compliance with a draft registration law may impinge certainly and immediately but unquantifiably on political or religious interests, whereas noncompliance may risk less certain and immediate but more measurable social, economic, and physical costs (disgrace, loss of employment, a fine, a prison sentence). Thus, in determining the importance of impacts, consideration is given to, among other things, whether they will be appraised in the short or the long term and whether more attention will be paid to impacts that are measurable or not measurable.

Some thinkers stop at this point and allow consequences and their impacts on interests to make the case for having factual rather than normative reasons determine whether to apply an applicable legal norm in a situation. Other thinkers go on to inquire not only about consequences and interests but also about consequences and values.

Values

Values sometimes mean the ideas in people's minds about what they want (their will) and sometimes the things that are wanted (the objects and the objectives of their will, which can be anything under, and even beyond, the sun). In the context of tension between respect for normative authority and judgments about what is prudent, values figure as a part of prudence as ideas rather than as objects. It is the fact of valuing, not what is being valued (which may not exist), that may be in tension with the authority of a legal norm. When A, having contracted to sell his ancestral home, Blackacre, to B, undergoes a change of mind and does not want to part with it, it is what A thinks about Blackacre, not Blackacre itself, that is in tension with the authority of A's contractual obligation to convey Blackacre to B. In short, the focus is on the mind of the value holder, and the valued object is incidental. Thus, compared with interests, one's concern with values is less with their content and more with their ranking. In fact, values are in large part simply the ranking of interests.

Value holders, like interest holders, may be individuals or groups. While groups do not, of course, actually have minds (although we often speak of the "will of the people"), the law allows individual agents to represent principals that are in fact groups;

and these agents may hold values in their minds on behalf of their principals. When the value holder is a state, or a corporation, or some other group with legally recognized agents, its values mean ideas in its agents' minds about what is wanted for the group. Individuals are free to desire for themselves what is not necessarily in their own interests, but agents are less free to want for a principal what is against its interests. Nevertheless, even concerning groups, interests and values are not identical. Agents may be empowered to want things for the group that are not limited by its interests: those representing states and corporations have the power to make "charitable" contributions for humanitarian reasons without having to justify them in terms of state or corporate interests, although they usually like to have such justifications available.

The prediction of consequences, assignment of interests, and assessment of impacts of consequences on interests can all be done more or less objectively, employing the logics of probability and utility. And impacts of consequences on values—including consequences of subjects or officials applying or not applying legal norms to their conducts—can also be objectively assessed once values have been defined. But values themselves, unlike interests, cannot be objectively assigned, because people can and do want what is neither probable nor useful. Thus, to give their values—their wants, aspirations, dreams—a semblance of subjective coherence, value holders seek to discover their values and to order them into value systems, hierarchies in their minds of their abstract values, in preparation for the countless occasions when they are called on to make situational value judgments. Value systems are, of course, developed for living, not just for dealing with legal problems, and value judgments about applying legal norms are but a small (but, I believe, identifiable) corner of the universe of value judgments.

An item in one's value system important to one's legal thinking is the abstract value, if any, placed on being law abiding and the ranking of this value relative to other values of the value holder. The higher the ranking, the less likely it is that there will be norm-value tension in determining whether to apply an applicable legal norm. Some other values, like those placed on keeping promises and telling the truth, also do not ordinarily create norm-value tension. But these exemplary moral values are outnumbered by a virtual infinity of possible values—possible exercises of will—that are likely to be in tension with normative authority (the definition of the word *willful* includes the idea of being unruly), including, prominently, values derived from ranking self-interests. We tend to want what we think will serve our interests, in rough relationship to the priorities we give these interests, without much attention to the rights, interests, or wants of others; and even our benign altruistic values can be in tension with legal norms, as when we seek to emulate Robin Hood by giving to others what does not belong to us.

Values lend themselves to being given priorities by or for the value holder more readily than do consequences or even interests. Values are internally adopted and accorded meaning and relative importance by exercises of one's own will, albeit exercises that are often seductively manipulated from outside. In contrast, consequences happen and interests accrue from external events willy-nilly; consequences by the workings, impervious to interests or values, of cause and effect (when you hit me, I hurt, regardless of whether I need or want to hurt); interests, as byproducts of one's positions and involvements in larger systems (legal systems that protect private property assign to all property owners, including those who do not value private property, interests in their property). All persons with the capacity to exercise free will are sovereign regarding their values, and how one defines and ranks what one values defines the kind of person one is. "Where your treasure is, there will your heart be also" Matthew 6:21—or, in more contemporary language, you are what you want.

Tension between law and value is experienced when there is a question as to whether the conduct of a value holder will be guided by an applicable legal norm or by the value. While the value may indicate either compliance or noncompliance with the norm, tension typically is felt when the value holder prefers not to comply, when the norm interferes with the value. The quality of the tension felt will be shaped by the abstract authority of this norm in the mind of the person, the abstract meaning and importance of this value in the person's value system, and the situational authority of the norm and the situational meaning and importance of the value when norm and value collide in this situation.

Returning to A, who had contracted to sell Blackacre to B, the legal norm is found in the contract. Now suppose that A's abstract values include, ranked in descending order, protecting the welfare and happiness of his family, protecting his own economic interests, keeping promises, and obeying the law, and that, since the execution of the contract to sell Blackacre, A's children have begged A not to let Blackacre pass out of the family. A's value of highest rank urges keeping Blackacre, even though values of lower rank urge conveying Blackacre to B. And A's lawyer advises that, because of the legal meaning of this norm, if B insists a court will order A to convey Blackacre to B (courts will order "specific performance" of contracts involving the sale of land and other "unique" property). Thus, if A is to act in accordance with his highest value, he will have to persuade B, perhaps with a substantial money settlement, not to insist on performance of the contract.

Points of View for Experiencing Norm-Fact Tension

Respect for normative authority and judgment about what is prudent—the contending forces that create norm-fact tension in a legal thinker's mind—possess general qualities that can be described regardless of who is experiencing the tension (although most of the discussion thus far has assumed the point of view of a subject). But an account of this tension also requires attention to the perspectives from which its forces are experienced. A subject of a legal system choosing whether to obey an applicable legal norm experiences norm-fact tension differently than does an official of that system deciding whether to enforce such a norm. But subjects and officials share an immediacy in what they experience that is lacking for those who advise them; and, for those who think as legislators or legal scholars, the norm-fact tension experienced is not tied to situations in which they are participants. This section examines how norm-fact tension is perceived from the points of view of subjects, of officials, and of those who experience it from the sidelines.

Subjects making choices about obeying applicable legal norms

Subjects are free to choose (to exercise their individual wills about) whether they obey or disobey applicable legal norms. In contrast, officials are faced not with free choices but with more circumscribed decisions: while not free to choose to disobey applicable laws, they often have power to decide—to make official judgments—regarding when such laws will be enforced. Thus, for subjects, applying applicable legal norms in legal situations has a special meaning. Being endowed with autonomous power over themselves and over no one else, subjects who apply legal norms choose to relinquish parts of their autonomy by acting as the norms direct, rather than as their own wills direct. In contrast, nonapplication for subjects means retaining and exercising autonomy by not accepting the authority of the norm to determine how they act. The powerlessness of subjects over others and subjects' unlimited freedom as to themselves combine to make subjects think less normatively and more factually than do officials or advisers. Subjects tend to see legal problems not as separate cases, as lawyers are trained to do, but rather as undifferentiated parts of life's complications: lawsuits, tax bills, and no-parking signs merge with marital difficulties, the common cold, and inclement weather to form some of the less appealing parts of one's view of the world. However, normative authority still has sufficient impact on most subjects for them to feel its tension with factual prudence. This subsection looks first at how the normative authority of the law is experienced from the perspective of being a subject of a legal system and then at how the countervailing force of the promptings of prudence is experienced from this perspective.

Subjects and authority

Not having assumed responsibility for maintaining a legal system's normative authority, subjects are free to choose for themselves whether or not particular legal norms, acknowledged to be applicable, will be treated as authoritative in particular situations. They may base their choices on categorical appraisals of authority made in advance (most drivers stop at red traffic lights) or on appraisals made contingently in view of the specifics of situations (more selectivity is exercised about obeying stop signs). Appraisals of authority may be affirmative, negative, or inconclusive and may focus on the legal, moral, or factual aspects of authority. And subjects may or may not act on appraisals of authority: they may acknowledge a norm's authority but not follow it (say, a stop sign), or deny a norm's authority but do as it directs (say, an expired contract), or simply act without thinking about the norm or its authority (say, the rule that one use due care). Some subjects, but not many, relinquish their freedom in advance and choose to respect the authority of all valid laws of their legal system in all situations in which such laws are applicable, come what may. They treat their status as subjects of a legal system as its officials are supposed to treat their offices. More commonly, subjects make ad hoc choices about whether they will respect the authority of particular norms in particular situations, with frequent case-by-case shifts as to the aspects of authority—legal, moral, factual—that are emphasized.

What are some of the reasons subjects may have for respecting the authority of a legal norm?

- Because it is the law—Subjects accept the legitimacy of the procedures by which the norm was adopted and believe that they should respect its authority simply because it is the law, whether or not they agree with the morality of its content and whether or not it is generally obeyed or enforced. And they might take this position as to this particular law even though they do not respect all laws (one who is scrupulous about paying his or her taxes may disobey "Don't Walk" signs).
- Because its content coincides with their own moral views—They respect a particular law because they see it as right and do not care about the dubious legitimacy of its origin (say, because it is a product of judicial legislation) or about how it is received by others. They may have a variety of standards for measuring what is right.
- Because it is obeyed and, more persuasively, because it is enforced—They respect the authority of a law that is generally

> treated as authoritative, particularly one that is so treated by enforcing officials; they leave speculative questions about legitimacy and morality to academics and clerics.

Conversely, subjects may reject a norm's authority because the procedures used to create it are dubious, because its content is repugnant to their moral views, or because it is not taken seriously by other subjects or by officials who are supposed to enforce it. And, of course, many subjects lack knowledge or interest concerning a norm's legitimacy, morality, or efficacy and, by default, base their choices to obey or disobey on prudence rather than on authority.

Subjects seldom hold strong views for or against a norm's legal authority because they seldom know or care about the legitimacy of its origins. And those who regard factual authority as crucial usually can make, or have made for them, reasonably firm predictions about compliance and enforcement. But subjects who focus on normative authority's moral aspects raise more complex problems because moral authority can have so many different and hard-to-define sources: community attitudes about right and wrong (what questions are community questions, and what is the relevant community?); ethical obligations attached to professions or positions (as determined by whom?); self-assumed obligations of individual conscience (to be proved how?); and broad ideals of justice and fairness (to be found where?). Of these kinds of moral authority, the most persuasive for most subjects are likely to be the attitudes of their own communities and the promptings of their own consciences.

It is not always possible to determine a subject's appraisal of a norm's authority from his or her conduct, because a person may choose, for other reasons, to act inconsistently with this appraisal. In order to maintain the authority of the legal system as a whole or in order simply to avoid trouble, one may follow a rule that seems—for legal, moral, or factual reasons—to be unauthoritative. Conversely, one may not follow a rule that seems legally authoritative because it conflicts with a religious norm (say, about sabbath observance) or because the cost of compliance in terms of one's interests or values seems prohibitive (say, when one's competitors are not subject to this rule). And, of course, one may act according to or not according to a legal rule without thinking one way or the other about its authority, as when one does not know or does not care about the existence of the rule or about its authority.

To perceive how particular subjects may view the normative authority of particular legal norms, consider the following situations:

- Sidney, an able-bodied eighteen-year-old man who would prefer not to perform military service, is confronted with a statute, recently upheld by a unanimous Supreme Court decision, requiring him to register for the draft.
- Susan, an unmarried pregnant woman who would prefer not to bear her child, is confronted with a Supreme Court decision by a divided court, with a strong dissenting opinion, upholding a statute in her home state that makes abortions in her situation illegal.
- Samson Industries, Inc., a corporation that would prefer to operate at a profit, is confronted with a binding contract with a customer that can be performed only at a substantial loss for Samson Industries.

Assume that these three subjects, while generally seeing themselves as law abiding, have not relinquished their freedom to choose when they will regard laws as authoritative. In these situations, what factors will they consider in making their appraisals of normative authority—legal, moral, and factual—and are such appraisals likely to determine how they will act?

Legal authority. Both Sidney and Samson Industries seem to have no grounds for questioning the legal authority of the legal norms confronting them: the constitutionality of the draft registration statute has been recently and decisively upheld, and the company's contract is described as binding. Susan can point to the split decision and strong dissent as diminishing the legal authority of the norms, state and federal, that combine to make the abortion she wants illegal in her home state. Even if she is generally law abiding, she may conclude that these laws do not call for the same respect, purely as laws, that other laws do. Thus, if she can afford it, she may feel free to have an abortion in another state with different abortion laws; she may even conclude that she can have an illegal abortion in her home state without becoming an outlaw.

Moral authority. Samson Industries seems to have scant grounds for questioning the moral authority of the contract. Possible moral arguments might be based on the unfairness of being held to what has turned out to be a one-sided contract (appeal to an ideal) and on any business mores that bargains of this sort should be renegotiated (appeal to a custom). However, the draft and abortion laws provide opportunities to question their moral authority, since they involve community attitudes, ethical obligations, individual conscience, and ideals of justice and fairness in the following ways:

- Social morality—Community attitudes generally support draft registration but are more divided about restrictions on abortions.
- Ethics—An able-bodied male citizen who enjoys the benefits of a society may have an ethical obligation to help defend it. A woman's ethical obligation to society to bear the child she has conceived is less clear.
- Conscience—Sidney's conscience may direct him either way, to respect the moral authority of the law to tell him his duty as a citizen or to deny its moral authority to force him to participate in war making. Or, as is more likely, Sidney's conscience may eschew patriotism and pacifism alike and leave him free to do whatever he thinks will least disrupt his life. Susan's conscience may not support the moral authority of the law to tell her what to do in this instance, because she sees what happens within her body as a personal rather than societal issue. And, while her conscience may make it difficult for her to have an abortion, it may do so with little or no deference to the law. Nevertheless, if her conscience clearly tells her that abortion is wrong, she may respect the moral authority of the law because it accords with her own conscience.
- Ideals—Are involuntary military service and involuntary motherhood just or fair? The moral authority of draft registration and abortion control laws can be supported by arguing that society needs soldiers and babies and that young men and women should take their fair chances of being called on to fill these needs. Or the moral authority of these laws can be attacked by questioning the need for more soldiers and babies than can be produced voluntarily and by arguing that, in any event, it is neither just nor fair to force people to become soldiers or mothers against their will if others, better placed in society, render these services only when they choose to do so. Thus, the morality of draft and abortion laws may depend on

whether they are needed and on whether they can be enforced evenhandedly.

Factual authority. Each of the three subjects will have questions about the factual authority—the efficacy—of the norms that confront them. If hundreds of thousands of other eighteen-year-olds have failed to register for the draft and if only a few of them have been prosecuted, Sidney has grounds for being unimpressed with the factual authority of the draft registration law. Similarly, if large numbers of women are having illegal abortions without legal repercussions, Susan will doubt the efficacy of the antiabortion law. (However, as noted later, Sidney and Susan may have prudential, as well as legal and moral, reasons for discounting the facts that the norms they confront are widely ignored by others.) While factual authority in Sidney's and Susan's cases is shaped by the conduct of other subjects and of enforcing officials, in Samson Industries' case the factual authority of the contract is largely in the hands of the company and the other contracting party; they can enhance it by abiding by or agreeing to modify the contract; they can diminish it by repudiating or ignoring the contract.

Authority and conduct. Suppose that Sidney chooses to register for the draft, Susan to have an illegal abortion in her home state, and Samson Industries to negotiate a settlement making the contract somewhat less costly. To what extent is each choice likely to be the result of respect or disrespect for normative authority?

- Sidney's choice to apply the legal norm in his situation would seem to be dictated in part by his realization that the draft law has clear legal authority and has strong, although less clear, moral authority, and in part by realization that it may be imprudent to rely on the seeming weakness of its factual authority because of the long-term risk of suffering the consequences of being branded a draft dodger (a risk that owes much to the norm's legal and moral authority).
- Susan's choice not to apply the legal norm to her situation seems less a result of an appraisal of its lack of normative authority than of a choice to be guided by prudence rather than by authority. While she may question the pedigree, morality, and efficacy of the abortion law, her choice probably rests on

the consequences to her own life of being the mother of an unwanted child. She would be less concerned than Sidney about the long-term risk of being exposed as a lawbreaker, in part because she would see herself as paying a higher price for compliance with the law (the probability of having the unwanted baby) than would Sidney (having his name go into the draft pool).

- Samson Industries' choice to compromise—neither to apply nor to reject the legal norm but rather to change it—reflects the clearest recognition of normative authority of these three hypothetical situations. Samson depends on general respect for the legal, moral, and factual authority of contracts for its own survival as a business corporation. Thus, its way out of a bad situation is to make this particular norm less burdensome, which, of course, is easier done with a contract than with a draft or abortion law.

Subjects and prudence

Authority concerns norms and their capacity to command respect. Prudence concerns thinkers making judgments about what is likely to happen to interests and values. Those who think as subjects tend to concentrate on consequences to their own interests and values and tend to value their own interests. Maintenance of normative authority and protection of interests and values other than their own they leave to others, on the sensible assumption that only subjects themselves can give their interests and values undivided attention and loyalty. To flesh out the prudential concerns of subjects, I will examine here how our three protagonists—Sidney, Susan, and Samson Industries—would think about the consequences of applying and of not applying the norms that confront them concerning, respectively, draft registration, abortion, and contract obligations. Then I will examine the interests and values likely to be affected by these consequences and how these subjects would be likely to appraise these impacts.

Consequences. Prudence starts with subjects predicting (sometimes aided by advisers) what is likely to happen if they do or do not apply applicable norms. In most general terms, if norms are applied, subjects are no longer free to do as they choose but are at peace with the law; if norms are not applied, subjects are free to choose what they do but risk legal and moral sanctions.

Subjects predict the consequences of both their compliance and their noncompliance with the norms. They think about such consequences both as direct happenings, independent of how other people react (a consequence of a subject obeying a speed limit may be that he or she will be late to work), and as reactions of other people (a consequence of a subject not obeying a speed limit may be that an official will decide to arrest him or her; a consequence of obeying may be that the subject's employer will be displeased). And subjects think about both short- and long-term happenings and reactions. As the illustration suggests, subjects tend to think in the short term both about what will happen to them if they comply with the law and about how others, particularly officials, will react if they do not.

For our protagonists, the most significant short-term direct happenings likely to result from compliance (and avoidable by noncompliance) are, respectively, that Sidney's name will go into the draft pool, that Susan will have her baby, and that Samson Industries will suffer financial loss by performing its contract—all happenings that they want to avoid. Longer-term happenings about which they may ponder are that Sidney may have to perform military service, that Susan will have a child for whom she is responsible, and that Samson will have to absorb its loss or go out of business. And, in the still longer term, the direct consequences of compliance may seem less dire: Sidney's military service may give him new confidence and skills; Susan may love and be loved by her child; Samson may prosper notwithstanding this contract.

Our subjects will also consider the reactions of other people to the subjects' noncompliance with the law. In the short term, Sidney and Susan risk legal prosecution and the moral opprobrium of some people (mitigated, perhaps, by the moral support of other people); and Samson risks a lawsuit that would probably cost more than would performance of the contract. Longer-term reactions include the following:

- Sidney may be sentenced to a prison term and a record of being a draft dodger may plague his future life, although some people may respect his refusal to cooperate with the draft.

- Susan also risks, less significantly than Sidney, official punishment and the danger of having her noncompliance with the law used against her in the future. But there may be countervailing positive reactions from those who support her choice.
- Samson Industries can expect damage to its business reputation and loss of confidence in the integrity of its contracts, although these reactions might be lessened if performance of the contract would hurt other creditors.

Subjects make these short- and long-term predictions about happenings and reactions that may result from compliance and noncompliance with legal norms as parts of their everyday lives. How they make them helps to define the qualities of the societies of which they are parts and their individual qualities as persons. But they do not predict consequences objectively, like weather forecasters, or even like other legal thinkers who are not thinking as subjects. They predict as self-interested, self-determined subjects.

Interests and values. Aside from our assumption—needed to create norm-fact tension—that our protagonists prefer not to apply the norms applicable in their situations, thus far we have assigned the subjects neither interests nor values. Consequences of compliance and noncompliance have been discussed without regard to how these subjects' needs or desires might be affected. But, as noted, subjects predict consequences not as exercises in forecasting but rather to measure how their self-interests and desires will fare. In fact, preoccupation with one's own welfare and priorities is a characteristic that sets a subject's legal thinking apart from other kinds of legal thinking.

The preceding section noted that the abstract interests typically involved in legal problems entail three kinds of interests: economic, involving money and other property; physical, involving well-being of body and psyche; and political, involving freedom and power. It also noted that, since individual subjects choose and assign priorities to what they want (which may or may not coincide with what they need), values and their rankings are internal and subjective, though susceptible to external influence and manipulation.

How Sidney's economic interests are likely to be affected by military service depends largely on his prospects as a civilian:

being drafted is less threatening economically to an unemployed laborer than to a person planning to study medicine. Nonetheless, one's economic prospects are not enhanced by prosecution for draft evasion or by a term in prison, possible consequences of noncompliance. And short-term economic losses from compliance may be offset by longer-term gains. Impacts of compliance on Sidney's physical interests depend on several contingencies, including whether he is drafted, the nature of his military service, and his luck in avoiding injury; and noncompliance carries its own psychological and physical hazards. Most insurers consider soldiers poorer risks than civilians but better risks, during peacetime, than convicts. Sidney's freedom would be diminished by military service, but less than it would be by going to prison, and military service may offer opportunities to exert legitimate power over others. How Sidney will evaluate these possible gains and losses (how he ranks being well-off, safe, free to do as he pleases, and powerful) and which values he cherishes that are independent of his interests (say, to be dutiful, honorable, or principled) will depend on how he structures his own value system.

Susan's short-term economic welfare, health, and freedom are all likely to suffer if she has an unwanted child to raise. However, the child, if allowed to be born, could provide longer-term offsetting benefits to Susan in the form of protection against destitution and loneliness. The danger that her noncompliance with this law will result in a criminal prosecution or a prison term is probably minimal. Compared with Sidney, Susan is likely to think less in terms of the substance of her interests—which to an observer may seem evenly balanced—and more in terms of how her own value system ranks what she wants. Whereas Sidney will probably see noncompliance with the draft law as entailing unacceptable threats to his interests in staying out of legal trouble (even though this interest may not be his highest value), Susan will probably see compliance with the abortion law as entailing unacceptable threats to her desire to keep her life free of the distractions and the economic and emotional claims of motherhood. She will reach this conclusion because her value system puts her interest in not having an unwanted child ahead of any interest that would be furthered by having a child (say, to enrich her life) and any disinterested desires she may have to obey the law or to obey a morality that treats a fetus as a human being.

Interests and values are more likely to coincide for Samson Industries than for Sidney or Susan. Samson is a business corporation organized to make profits for its owners; its managers are legally and ethically obligated to want for it what will further its economic interests. Their problem is the relatively uncomplicated one of making a business judgment regarding how these interests will be best served in the face of a costly contract. No one is likely to go to jail, whether they opt in good faith for compliance, noncompliance, or settlement. It is dishonorable for a business enterprise to fail to keep a commitment; but it is even worse, by honoring one commitment, to cause the enterprise to default on other commitments with equal claims to its assets. In the discussion of authority and conduct, it was suggested that Samson would probably seek to negotiate a change in the terms of the contract, a prudent middle course between repudiation and performance.

Each of the three subjects wants to avoid applying an applicable legal norm. While their value judgments can result from the ranking of interests, they can also, as discussed, result independent of, and even despite, interests. Sidney might refuse to register for the draft simply because he wants to stay clear of any cooperation with war making. Susan might refuse to have her child simply because she does not want to bring another child into what she sees as an overpopulated or a doomed world. Samson's managers might repudiate the contract simply because they do not want to injure their other creditors. And opposite choices are also explainable solely in terms of values: Sidney might register because he wants to do his duty as a citizen; Susan might have her baby because she wants one; and Samson might perform its contract because its managers want, on behalf of Samson, to keep its promises. But then, of course, the tension between norm and fact relaxes, because the norm and the ranking value point to the same result and the ranking value overcomes any interests or other values that point to another result.

Officials making decisions about applying applicable legal norms

Tension in legal thinking between respecting normative authority and judging what is prudent is of a quite different quality for officials than it is for subjects. Officials have clearer, more compelling obligations to respect the authority of legal norms. And, while the process of forecasting consequences does not intrinsically differ for officials and subjects (since both deal with objective, cause-and-effect connections), questions about whose interests and values are at stake pose special problems for officials. Subjects are free to limit their thinking to how their own interests and values are likely to be affected by applying or not applying legal norms. Lacking this focus on concrete self-interests and desires, officials grapple with elusive public interests and values, which are sometimes lumped under the rubric of public policy. And officials are supposed to keep their official views of public policy separate not only from what they need and want for themselves but also frequently from what they, as individuals, want for society and from their own perceptions of social needs and wants. (For example, judges accept the public policies of legislatures and higher courts, and sometimes of administrative agencies, although such policies may not be what the judges would choose or perceive as needed.) Subjects are allowed and even expected to put themselves first when thinking about legal problems; officials, however, are supposed to put themselves out of the picture. Whether one expects officials also to put out of the picture their own aspirations for and perceptions of the public welfare depends on the offices they hold, the norms they are deciding whether to apply, and how one views normative authority.

Officials take oaths to respect the normative authority of all valid norms of their legal systems and often are literally clothed with indicia of this authority—by the robes, uniforms, and badges they wear and the insignias on their vehicles. When acting as officials, they personify the law. They are supposed to respect the authority of a legal norm simply because it is the law, whether or not they agree with the morality or efficacy of its content, although they may have more leeway when they have doubts about the legitimacy of the procedures used to create it or about whether it is taken seriously by other officials, especially by their own superiors.

There is disagreement regarding the extent to which officials do and should temper, or even replace, their respect for normative authority by considerations of public policy. On the one hand, some argue that determination and implementation of public policy (politics) form the province of elected legislators, and that while officials (who usually are appointed rather than elected) may sometimes defer to public policy in terms of legislative purpose when they are interpreting legal norms, they are not supposed to defer to their own perceptions of public policy when applying legal norms. On the other hand, others argue that most official legal decisions are political decisions about the use of governmental power, and that the logical applicability of norms to events—that is, the legal reasoning that gives normative authority its coherence—is an illusion fostered by law professors, judges, and lawyers. A middle position acknowledges that mechanical application of all logically applicable norms to events is neither possible nor desirable but argues that it does not necessarily follow that all official decisions are political or that legal reasoning is an empty pretense of the legal mind. The extreme positions would, each in its own way, deny the existence of norm-fact tension at the application stage of a legal problem, since they argue, respectively, that factual considerations (beyond those already weighed to determine applicability) are irrelevant, or that normative considerations (beyond providing legal cover for political decisions) are illusory. To me, the middle position seems the most persuasive—and it will also allow this chapter to proceed.

While subjects have differing attitudes toward, and experiences of, tension between normative authority and factual prudence, they all view this tension from much the same vantage point in a legal system. And subjects experience the commands of authority in similar ways; differences occur in the ways in which they use prudence to modify how they react to these commands in order to accommodate their own interests and values. In contrast, there are different kinds of officials, and their differences derive quite directly from their different functions and authorities in a legal system, mainly from whether they are judges or enforcement officials. And, since no officials are supposed to use prudence to modify their respect for the commands of authority in order to accommodate other than public interests and values, there is little point in examining an official's relations to authority and prudence, as was done with subjects. Rather, separate examination is made here of how judges and enforcement officials experience norm-fact tension as they decide whether to apply applicable legal norms in legal situations.

Judges

Norm-fact tension in the minds of judges, as compared with that in the minds of enforcement officials, is characterized by a strong presumption in favor of respect for normative authority over prudential concern for consequences to public interests and values. Particularly for appellate judges, this presumption is reinforced by an Olympian remoteness from the practical aspects of legal problems: from the events involved, from the consequences of applying norms to events, and from the need to take initiatives in resolving legal problems. They sit above the battle, rendering judgments only when called upon, on the basis of sacred, preordained laws—or so it seems.

The judicial presumption favoring authority over prudence has been considered a necessary part of governments based on laws, as distinguished from governments that put the will of those in power or the dictates of economic theories or religious doctrines above the law. While judges do take into account weaknesses in the legal authority of a norm (as when it derives from a decision by a closely divided court or from a decision that subsequent decisions have refused to extend beyond its facts) and do seek ways to avoid applying a norm that has lost its moral or factual authority (for example, a norm that forbids certain attire in public or one that requires seals on documents), judges are supposed generally to assume that a norm with a proper legal pedigree is entitled to respect. Furthermore, judges are not supposed to use public policy as a reason for replacing old laws with new ones, because determination and implementation of policy is supposed to be left to legislators. And, since most appellate judgments must be publicly justified in written decisions, judges often turn to normative authority to support their decisions, since this provides justifications that seem less controversial than those provided by as yet unlegislated policy. Of course, to the extent that policy is written into law, the tension between norm and policy abates and obedience and prudence merge.

Ordinarily, the legal problems that come before judges have already been screened and narrowed by other officials and by subjects and their advisers. Factual uncertainties are minimized for trial judges by presuit investigations, pretrial discovery proceedings, stipulations, and jury verdicts. Before judges must make final decisions, most cases have been settled (often with judicial mediation, since judges can be more relaxed about normative authority in the privacy of their chambers). Even further removed from the fray than trial judges are appellate judges to whom cases come with neatly packaged findings of fact and a few isolated questions of law to be decided. Under the Anglo-American adversary system of litigation, the role of trial and appellate judges is to react to the initiatives of the parties and their advisers. Judges generally try to decide as little as possible on the narrowest, least controversial grounds available. And judges are isolated, personally and professionally, from the pressures of politics and the marketplace. Not being called on to make or justify policy or to attract or serve clients, judges are positioned to concentrate their minds and wills, without fear or favor, on protecting and enhancing the law's integrity, coherence, and authority.

Skeptics argue that this picture of judges does not accord with reality (see, for example, the picture painted by Charles Dickens in *Bleak House*). Some claim that judges cannot avoid being in politics, because they obtain (and sometimes keep) their offices through political connections and, more significantly, because their decisions affect how power is distributed in our society—even though these decisions may be justified in terms of the commands of normative authority. On a more idealistic level, those who see law only as an instrument for achieving good consequences, and not as a good in itself, point out that the great judges have been activists who were willing to create new law and who tempered respect for normative authority with regard for the public welfare. It should be noted, however, that great judges have generally exercised their courage and initiative at the stage at which legal norms are being interpreted, rather than at the stage at which norms of accepted meaning are being applied. For a judge to refuse to apply an applicable legal norm on grounds of policy or expediency is an affront to its normative authority, whereas when a judge is able to find, or have found for him or her, a construction of the norm that avoids its application in the case, this affront is avoided. To argue that judges are free to be result oriented at the application stage is to argue that they are, in effect, little different from enforcement officials.

Enforcement officials

Situations in which regulatory or criminal laws are normatively applicable are so numerous that full enforcement is impracticable: observe any major highway or almost any criminal courtroom in the United States. Thus, in addition to judges, most legal systems have another, much larger corps of officials who are empowered to select situations in which enforcement of applicable norms is to be sought. They select both the norms that are to be enforced and the subjects who are to be subjected to enforcement (although with civil norms, as well as some regulatory and criminal norms, the initiative in selecting situations for application is left to aggrieved subjects). Police officers, prosecuting attorneys, and enforcement staffs of regulatory agencies all serve as enforcement officials; ministerial officials, regarding the norms entrusted to them, contribute to enforcement by considering whether to overlook deviations, by negotiating with subjects about compliance, and by recommending enforcement proceedings. Out-of-court decisions about applications of norms are also enabled by statutes that empower government agencies to make, interpret, and enforce their own rules in specialized areas, and by the availability for civil disputes of contractual means of resolution, such as settlement and arbitration.

Two different sets of norms contend with prudential concerns in the minds of enforcement officials: the norms of substantive law that officials are supposed to enforce governing the conduct of subjects, and the norms (commonly designated due process) of constitutional and procedural law that officials are supposed to respect governing the rights of subjects and the conduct of officials. Enforcement officials have less than complete respect for the authority of these two sets of norms for different reasons. With substantive norms, lack of respect is largely the result of the sheer number of norms and violations to be dealt with. With due process norms, to which officials are themselves subjects, the norms are often seen by officials as impediments to the performance of their duty to enforce the substantive norms entrusted to them. Having selected and developed situations for enforcement (a process frequently entailing lengthy investigation), some officials may seek to justify their labors by winning their cases without being inhibited by the niceties of due process.

Prudential concerns that contend with normative authority in the minds of enforcement officials include three kinds, one legitimate and two illegitimate. Because all legal norms cannot be enforced in all situations in which they are applicable, it is legitimate for officials to select situations for enforcement on the basis of public policy. (O, a police officer, may arrest A and not B for speeding because A's violation is more dangerous than B's; and, also on this basis of public safety, O may enforce a drunk-driving law more strictly than a speed limit.) But, in making these selections, officials cannot legitimately consider consequences to their own interests or values. (In arresting A and not B when both violate the same law, O may not do so because A exhibits a lifestyle of which O disapproves or because B is O's brother; nor may O be easier on speeding than on drunken driving because O is a teetotaling car racing enthusiast.) And it is not legitimate for officials to consider consequences to any interests or values, public or private, in determining whether applicable norms about the due process rights of subjects will be applied. (Having selected A for arrest on the legitimate basis of public safety, O may not deny A due process because A is a public menace, or because O disapproves of A's lifestyle, or for any other reason.)

In selecting cases for enforcement and then trying to win them, it is not easy for officials to keep clear whether the motivating interests or values are the public's or their own; nor is it easy to keep separate whether officials are applying substantive norms to others or constitutional norms to themselves. Strong-minded officials tend to equate public policy with their own needs and wants, often with the result that how norms are enforced depends on who is in power. (For example, officials who cherish economic growth above clean air and water are likely to enforce environmental protection laws differently than officials with different priorities.) And conscientious officials tend to equate their own needs and wants with the substantive policy served by the norms they enforce, often with the result that the seeming strength of this policy in their minds obscures the constitutional rights of subjects. (For example, officials who enforce drug laws may come to feel that the end of convicting drug dealers justifies using unconstitutional means.)

Enforcement officials may also have difficulty knowing with precision which public policy they are supposed to be serving and which selections of cases for enforcement will best further that policy. While statements about public interests and values are sometimes found in preambles to and legislative histories of statutes, much of the content of public policy is left unexpressed. Police officers and prosecuting attorneys seldom have staffs to develop structures of policy considerations about the broad range of criminal laws they enforce. Traditional criminal laws—outlawing murder, assault, theft—are based on long-recognized societal needs and wants, and legislators are understandably reluctant to acknowledge formally the need or value of official discretion concerning when they will be enforced. Thus, when criminal law enforcement officials use public policy to select cases for enforcement they often simply refer to their own, or their superiors', perception of what the public needs and wants.

In some areas of regulatory norms and administrative law, less subjective methods have been developed that enable officials who enforce particular categories of legal norms to create objective structures that identify, and provide situational illustrations of, the public interests and values to be served. For example, Congress created the Securities and Exchange Commission (SEC) to administer and enforce a group of federal statutes regulating the securities business. The history and content of these statutes indicate that the policy they seek to further is the public need and desire for disclosure of material facts when someone is asked to buy or sell a security or to vote as a security holder. Over the years, these statutes have been supplemented and particularized by SEC rules and interpreted by the SEC and the federal courts. This body of rules and interpretations serves not only to clarify the normative meaning, abstract and situational, of federal securities legislation but also to illustrate, refine, and even modify how public interests and values are served in requiring disclosure of material facts in securities transactions. These illustrations, refinements, and modifications have dealt with public needs and wants in terms of such questions as: What kinds of transactions call for disclosure? What form and quantity of disclosure are needed and wanted? And, probably the hardest question, what information is to be considered material in a securities transaction? Thus, when SEC officials decide that the norms entrusted to them will be applied in specific situations, they draw on a structure of policy considerations in securities regulation. While SEC officials—monitored by the federal courts—continue to work to further the policy of disclosure, from time to time they change not only their interpretations of the meaning and the normative authority of the norms they enforce but also their own views about how much and what kind of disclosure public interests and values seem to require. Their administrative creation of a structure of policy considerations about disclosure resembles the process of judicial creation of the more strictly legal structures that we call the common law.

Views from the sidelines: Advisers, legislators, legal scholars

Only subjects and officials actually choose or decide whether to apply applicable legal norms in real-life situations. But they are often assisted in their choices or decisions by advisers, typically lawyers, who experience vicariously some of their clients' norm-fact tension. Furthermore, tension between the stability of normative authority and keeping law relevant to what is needed and wanted pervades the legislative process. And finally, teachers and commentators, as they seek to explain how a legal system works, experience tension over whether to give primacy to what normative authority says or to what participants in the system do.

Advisers: Tension experienced vicariously

Because advisers of subjects and officials do not themselves make choices or decisions about the application of norms to events, the norm-fact tension they experience is vicarious. And since subjects and officials relate differently to norms and facts, the norm-fact tension known by their respective advisers is different. But most advisers share two characteristics: the preference of lawyers to advise about legal rather than economic or social consequences; and the obligation of agents to act for and be loyal to their principals. However, as noted later, it is easier for advisers of subjects to know their principals and their needs and wants than it is for advisers of officials. While most advisers of officials are themselves officials, for our purposes here officials will be confined to those who themselves decide whether to apply norms.

Advisers participate in clients' choices and decisions in several ways. Lawyers' expertise often has already helped to conceptualize the legal situations that establish that norms are applicable and can now help to clarify their normative authority. Legal advice can help determine the legitimacy of procedures followed in a norm's creation and its efficacy in commanding respect, particularly of officials, but is less helpful in weighing its moral authority. On the prudential side, reliability of predictions about consequences is enhanced by the assistance of objective, uninvolved advisers; such advisers are also useful in calculating costs and benefits of predicted impacts on individual and group interests and in ranking these interests; and, while advisers are of less help with values than with consequences and interests, they can assist in ranking values and can advise value holders of the costs of giving values priority over norms and interests.

Subjects are free to focus on their own needs and wants and, if willing to suffer the consequences, to disregard both normative authority and the needs and wants of others. Their advisers, however, do not share this freedom to be single-minded. Advisers of subjects owe their first duty to their clients' welfare and wishes, but there are limits to how free they are to close their minds, either to normative authority or to what disobedience might do to other people. While lawyers disagree on the formulation of these limits, most agree that a conscientious lawyer will make clear to a client how the law directs subjects to act in the situation at hand; what is likely to happen—to the client, the law, and other people—if the client does or does not act that way; and that the choice is the client's, not the lawyer's. When the lawyer is convinced that disobedience will substantially and disproportionately impair the authority of the law or the interests and values, private or public, of other people, the lawyer will also make clear that a choice of disobedience will cause the lawyer to cease to represent the client. Thus, advisers often face more complex norm-fact (and fact-fact) tensions than do subjects.

In putting their clients' welfare and wishes first, advisers should refrain from advising subjects not only if the advisers' own interests may be affected by what subjects choose to do but also if the advisers' own strongly held values may color their advice. For example, it might be unfortunate for Sidney to receive legal advice about draft registration from an ardent pacifist, or Susan about an abortion from an antiabortionist, or Samson Industries about its unfortunate contract from one who gives highest priority to keeping promises. While pacifism, right-to-life views, and promise keeping may be admirable virtues for subjects to choose to live their own lives by—and perhaps even for legislators to impose on subjects—they should not be imposed on subjects by advisers who are supposed to be legal champions, not moral standard setters, for their clients.

Advisers of subjects seldom have trouble identifying their clients and the private interests and values they serve, or in separating the choices that subjects make from advising about such choices; but they often do have problems about how much attention they should pay to normative authority and to the interests and values of others. And this condition is more or less the same for all advisers of subjects. In contrast, advisers of officials have clear duties to respect normative authority (to which officials owe their offices) and to be attentive to public interests and values (the criteria officials are supposed to use in selecting cases for enforcement). But it is often difficult for advisers to identify whom they represent and to separate the deciding done by officials from advising about that deciding: the line between principal and agent becomes indistinct because both officials and their advisers are agents of the state. And the public interests and values that officials and their advisers are supposed to serve are less knowable than are the particular interests and values of an individual subject (even when the subject is a large corporation).

The jobs of advising judges and enforcement officials are quite different. Judges are expected to respect normative authority to extents impossible for enforcement officials, and enforcement officials are expected to concern themselves with public policy to extents improper for judges. Advisers of judges find normative authority set forth in law books—in statutes, rules, precedents, and commentaries. Advisers of enforcement officials, lacking comparable identifiable sources of public policy to use in selecting situations to recommend for enforcement, are often largely occupied in making ad hoc recommendations about who should be favored or disfavored. For example, if Sidney chooses not to register for the draft and Susan chooses to have an illegal abortion, joining many thousands of others in violation of the draft and abortion laws, what public policy standards are available to determine whether the cases of Sidney and Susan should be selected for enforcement? The amount of publicity Sidney gave to his refusal to register and how far Susan's pregnancy had progressed at the time of her abortion might be considered relevant to the general good to be accomplished by enforcement action in these cases, but in practice these decisions are likely to be left to "official discretion," with officials and advisers understandably reluctant to discuss how they separate the goats they select for prosecution from the sheep that will be left alone.

Legislators: Tension between the law's stability and its relevance

Legislators do not choose, decide, or advise about whether applicable legal norms will be applied in legal situations. For reasons and on occasions they themselves pick, they determine whether new legal norms will be created—usually in order to bring what the law requires more in line with what seems moral or prudent. And they usually legislate not to resolve situations already in progress but to provide general rules for future situations.

The norm-fact tension of legislators is between conservative reluctance to allow law to become a reflection of transient perceptions of interests and values and progressive impatience with allowing law to lose touch with what seems to be currently needed or wanted. This tension between concern for the law's stability and for its relevance differs from tension felt by other legal thinkers because legislators, within the limits of their legislative powers, are above the law in the sense that they can change it. The circumstance that a norm tells one to do X while prudence tells one to do Y does not create the same sort of tension for legislators as it does for other legal thinkers, because legislators are empowered to yield to prudence and to make Y the norm, whereas those who lack this power can do Y only by being scofflaws or derelict in their duties. The legislative act is a temporary victory of prudence over authority: a victory, because a part of existing normative authority is unseated (the norm is changed), and temporary, because what is prudent becomes what is the norm, so that in the next similar situation the norm will prevail. Once legislators act to change what the law requires—to sacrifice legal stability for legal relevance—norm and fact cease to contend with each other and begin to work together. Legislation is a way to encourage people (by ordering them) to do what seems prudent (like wearing seat belts in automobiles); and what seems prudent points the way to legislators in determining what should be legislated.

Chapter 1 divides legislators into, on the one hand, formal legislators (legislative bodies and their delegates) vested with general lawmaking powers and, on the other, subjects and officials who, less formally and more situationally, also create norms (subjects by their contracts, conveyances, incorporations, marriages, and the like; officials by their judicial, administrative, and ministerial decisions that create precedents for future decisions). Formal legislators legislate prospectively and, except for isolated "private acts," abstractly. In contrast, informal legislators can legislate retrospectively or prospectively and situationally or abstractly; but, lacking formal power to create new legal norms of general application, they legislate only as they are permitted by existing legal norms—they can create new law but can displace old law only when it is of their own making.

Legislators can be classified not only by the formality with which they legislate but also by whether they legislate for the state or for themselves. This latter classification is useful in examining how legislators balance their respect for existing norms with their desire that norms serve current needs and wants. Legislators for the state—members of legislatures and their delegates, and judges and other officials who legislate informally by establishing and changing precedents—are supposed to take into account the stability and coherency of the legal system they serve and to do their legislating in the public interest. There is, however, disagreement about whether they should legislate only what legislators for the state think the public needs, or whether they also should take into account what the public wants or what legislators want for the public. While honorable state legislators do not legislate in their own interests, they do sometimes legislate to promote special interests that they value—say, to protect the wilderness or to open up new areas for development. In contrast, those who legislate for themselves—subjects who make contracts and create other new legal relationships—are expected to be serving their own interests or values and are not expected to have concern for the legal system beyond the concern that flows from their own needs and wants.

Those who legislate for a legal system hold ultimate legal power within that system: power to change its norms, to turn what is legal into what is illegal, and vice versa. While they can less readily change the moral and factual contexts of legal norms, legislation is seldom without moral and factual consequences. Thus, when legislators change the law, norm-fact and other tensions of other legal thinkers change because, suddenly, they are playing by new rules and, less suddenly, they are operating in a new moral and factual environment. For example, legislation that limits or expands requirements for legal abortions changes all of the kinds of tension we have been considering: between structures and freedom in determining what the law requires, between law and morals in determining what one ought to do, and between norms and facts in determining what one will do. And these changes affect the legal thinking of many people, including women with unwanted pregnancies, their doctors and lawyers, their parents and husbands, putative fathers of the unborn children, enforcement officials and judges, those who advise the foregoing, future legislatures, and even legal scholars who teach or write about the law.

Legal scholars: Tension between concepts and functions

Being nonparticipating observers—without the capacity to obey, enforce, adjudicate, advise about, or change the law, but with the capacity to try to explain it—legal scholars experience a norm-fact tension that is even more abstract and detached than that experienced by legislators. The tension of legal scholars arises over how they themselves are to perceive, understand, and communicate what participating legal thinkers do when they change the law and deal with legal situations. This tension is mainly about whether they will cast their explanations as one would explain a normative system that is constituted and defined by its rules (say, a description of the game of chess), or as one would explain something happening in nature with emphasis on data rather than on rules (say, an account of the playing of a particular chess game).

Since few legal scholars view law as wholly normative or as wholly factual, and since their explanations are usually confined to norms and situations in particular fields, their tension is likely to be experienced as uncertainty over whether to focus on what norms in that field seem to require (concepts) or on what participants in that field actually do (functions) in light of consequences, interests, and values. For example, will one who teaches or writes about tax law emphasize what is said in the Internal Revenue Code, the Regulations, and decided cases, or what is done by taxpayers, their advisers, the Internal Revenue Service, and the courts? In explaining tax law, does one focus on understanding logical connections between complex rules, and often even more complex events, or on predicting how interests and values, private and public, are likely to be served or disserved? Variants of this kind of norm-fact tension have been labeled "conceptualism versus functionalism," "legal positivism versus legal realism," and "formalism versus critical legal studies." Other legal thinkers—who do not have to explain, but only to choose, decide, advise, or legislate—are less afflicted by this kind of tension, although something akin to it is experienced by judges when they seek to justify their decisions in hard cases in which normative authority and public policy seem to conflict.

Legal scholars begin their work by forming mental pictures of what legal norms require and what legislators and participants in legal situations do. These pictures are formed by reading constitutions, statutes, rules, contracts, judicial opinions, commentaries; by recalling their own experiences as subjects, officials, advisers, legislators; and by imagining variations of the norms and situations revealed by their reading and experience. With these pictures in mind, they struggle to understand why and how legislators legislate and what choices and decisions subjects and officials and their advisers are faced with and how they respond in legal situations. It is mainly at this stage, of understanding the creation of legal norms and their applicability and application to events, that norm-fact tension enters the thinking of legal scholars. Those who prize coherency may be tempted to ground their understanding on creation in their minds of an orderly, albeit sometimes complex, normative structure, like a chessboard with its squares and its pieces and their permitted moves. But, because law differs from chess (and from games in general) in that it must tolerate substantial noncompliance with its rules by both subjects and officials, there is a countervailing temptation to ground understanding on what participants in a legal system actually do for prudential reasons, rather than on what legal norms tell them to do.

For example, suppose a legal scholar thinks about people who have formed corporations in order to protect their individual assets from being at risk in business enterprises but who must confront efforts to impose the corporations' liabilities on them personally. Some of these efforts succeed and some do not. How are these different results to be understood? The major norm involved, that shareholders of legally formed corporations are not liable for corporate debts, seems to require officials to reject all efforts to impose personal liability. But suppose that some of the corporations were provided with assets that were arguably inadequate to meet probable liabilities, and some were operated as mere alter egos of controlling shareholders. Suppose further that the scholar discovers that judges in state A consider adequacy of the capitalization of corporations a question for the legislature but impose personal liability on shareholders when the corporations have acted as agents of the shareholders, thus invoking another legal norm (that a principal is liable for debts contracted for the principal by its agents) to justify not applying the norm of corporation law that limits liability to corporate assets. But the scholar also discovers that, on grounds of public policy, judges in state B simply disregard the protected status of shareholders of corporations that have what the judges consider to be inadequate capital, and that in doing so, the judges do not see themselves as trespassing on the province of the legislature. Thus, the scholar would have different understandings of what constitutes limited liability in states A and B—the former based on the normative authority of the law, the latter on public policy—and these understandings would be difficult to reconcile if the scholar was trying to unequivocally state the law on this point.

This illustration of how norm-fact tension may arise in the understanding stage of legal scholarship also shows the similarity mentioned earlier between this tension and that felt by judges as they seek to justify their decisions. But there are important differences between the positions of judges and scholars. Judges decide real cases and seek to justify their decisions by appeals to normative authority or public policy. Scholars are called on not to justify but rather to explain. From their perceptions of norms and events, they are expected first to form pictures of legal situations and then to understand these situations by imposing some sort of order—normative, prudential, or a combination of both—on the materials of which these situations are constituted, and finally, somehow to communicate that understanding. Scholars do not share the obligations of judges to respect normative authority and to leave legislation to the legislators, nor do they share the obligations of judges to keep the law consistent with public interests and values. The obligation of legal scholars is to perceive, understand, and communicate as clearly as they are able how a legal system works (an effort also likely to reveal how the system and the way it works can be improved). Thus, the norm-fact tension they experience is not over whether authority or prudence shall prevail but over whether authority or prudence better explains what happens. In the previous example regarding the corporation, authority seems to provide the better explanation in state A and prudence in state B. This illustration is useful because normative and factual explanations can be separated quite readily. In many situations, however, norms and facts do not disentangle this easily. But trying to sort out the promptings of authority and of prudence, in legislation as well as in legal situations, helps to make legal scholarship challenging.

After a legal scholar perceives and understands the options presented to legislators, subjects, officials, and advisers and the determinations they make, his or her task is to communicate this understanding to students or readers. At this point, a final distinction should be emphasized between teaching and writing. Teachers meet classes at scheduled times, before which they must have completed their class preparation, formed their mental pictures of legislation and situations, struggled to understand what the legal thinkers participating therein have done and what relative weight has been given to authority and prudence, and planned how they will communicate this understanding. While what happens in classrooms can change methods of communication and sometimes even the understanding of legal problems, the communication is usually quite separate from the perception and understanding that precede it. In contrast, the effort to write precisely often illuminates perception and understanding: the picture changes, an understanding of what participants are doing sharpens and deepens, and basic tensions in participants' minds between authority and prudence—along with antecedent tensions between structures and freedom and between law and morals—emerge from the background. While the different demands and tempos of teaching and writing make them difficult to do concurrently, and while proficiency in one does not guarantee proficiency in the other, the differences between them enable the two experiences to inform and enhance each other; teaching provides exposure to many and various legal problems, abstract and situational, while writing provides the imperative to think rigorously and to communicate carefully about these problems.

INDEX